I'm No Angel

Kylie Bisutti

I'M NO Angel

From **Victoria's Secret Model** to Role Model

Tyndale House Publishers, Inc.
Carol Stream, Illinois

Visit Tyndale online at www.tyndale.com.

TYNDALE and Tyndale's quill logo are registered trademarks of Tyndale House Publishers, Inc.

I'm No Angel: From Victoria's Secret Model to Role Model

Designed by Jacqueline L. Nuñez

Edited by Stephanie Rische

The author is represented by Chip MacGregor of MacGregor Literary Inc., 2373 NW 185th Avenue, Suite 165, Hillsboro, OR 97124.

ISBN 978-1-4143-8309-5

Printed in the United States of America

19	18	17	16	15	14	13
7	6	5	4	3	2	1

To my Lord and Savior, Jesus Christ. May this book be for Your glory. I am thankful for Your unending love and grace!

To Mikey, the love of my life. Thank you for loving me like Christ loves the church. Thank you for always showing me grace and for your prayers. You are my best friend, and I am absolutely blessed to be able to call you my husband and my partner in life. My greatest gift outside of knowing Christ and receiving His gift of love and salvation is knowing you.

To my mom and dad. Thank you both for pouring into my life and loving me. Thank you for modeling lives of character and integrity. And thank you for teaching me how to hunt and fish! I'm grateful to the Lord for all He has done in your lives, and I love who you have become in Christ.

To Papa and Grams. I cannot imagine my life without you. Thank you for all the time you spent with me as a little girl. Thank you for always being there for me. My heart rejoices knowing that I share such a bond with both of you.

CONTENTS

PROLOGUE

Charm is deceptive, and beauty is fleeting;
    but a woman who fears the LORD is to be praised.
PROVERBS 31:30

I'LL NEVER FORGET finding that first tweet just after Thanksgiving 2011:

Oh great . . . the Victoria's Secret Fashion Show . . . another reason not to eat.

It was followed almost immediately by another.
Then another.
And another.
All over the country, teenage girls and young women were taking to their Twitter accounts to pour out their angst and frustration over how they didn't measure up—how they felt physically inadequate in every area, from their weight to their appearance to their bust size.

Then, out of nowhere, amid all the anxiety and insecurity, came the tweet that would change my life forever:

I'd rather have a Proverbs 31 woman than a VS model.

The words came from Alex Eklund, the founder of Live 31, an organization committed to helping women gain a healthy, biblical self-image.

I couldn't help but smile. *Would anyone believe this is exactly my journey?* I wondered.

Then I tweeted:

I quit being a VS model to become a Proverbs 31 wife.

Little did I know what that single sentence would lead to. Within minutes, Alex contacted me and asked if I'd be interested in writing a blog post for his website, sharing my story.

I'd never spoken publicly about giving up my career as a lingerie model to become the woman God wanted me to be, but I felt like God was nudging me to do this. I said yes.

Later that evening I sat down at my computer and started writing.

I QUIT VICTORIA'S SECRET TO BE A PROVERBS 31 WIFE

I started my modeling career at the very young age
of fourteen. It was always my dream to become a
supermodel, and to be a Victoria's Secret model
was my ultimate goal. . . .

As I typed the final words of the blog post, I thought, *Well, if my modeling career wasn't over before, it will be now.* And yet I had total peace about my decision. I knew it was the right message—and hopefully one that might help free others who were trapped in a world of insecurity, self-loathing, eating disorders, and emptiness—a world I was all too familiar with.

I wanted no part of it anymore.

This is career suicide, I thought, hitting the Send button.

Chapter 1

ALL THINGS FOR GOOD

We know that in all things God works
for the good of those who love him, who
have been called according to his purpose.

ROMANS 8:28

FEBRUARY 7, 2012

"Dad just texted me again." My husband, Mike, glanced up from his phone, shaking his head in surprise. "He says Dr. Phil called. Anderson Cooper wants you on his show. Rosie O'Donnell wants to talk to you, and someone from *Inside Edition* just left a message for you at the house."

What's going on? I wondered. *Why is everyone suddenly so interested in me?*

Before I could even finish my thought, my phone rang. It was my agent, Sabrina.

"Kylie, where are you?" She sounded a little frantic.

"I'm in Fargo, North Dakota, with Mike. What's going on? All these talk shows and news outlets keep calling Mike's dad, looking for me."

"You're all over the news, Kylie!" Sabrina sounded shocked that I had no idea what was happening.

I'd been traveling with Mike on business, and we hadn't been online or watched much TV for the past few days. Besides, it had been months since I'd stopped modeling. I figured the media had completely forgotten about me—and frankly, I was fine with that.

"Apparently the interview you did with FoxNews.com about quitting Victoria's Secret to become a Proverbs 31 wife went live today. It's all over the news, and *Good Morning America* has offered to fly you to New York today so you can be on their show tomorrow morning." She paused, waiting for me to respond. I just stared at Mike, stunned.

"Kylie? How soon can you get to an airport?"

I caught a glimpse of my reflection in the front window. Dressed in a puffy ski coat and hunting boots, with no makeup and my hair pulled back in a ponytail, I was about as far from media ready as I could get. And there wasn't a single thing in my suitcase that was going to be an improvement.

"Well . . . we're about four hours from the nearest airport," I said. "And I really didn't bring anything with me that I could wear on TV."

"That's okay," Sabrina assured me. "Just get yourself on a plane. When you arrive, we can shop for something appropriate. I'll bring a few backup outfits just in case. See you in a few hours." And before I even could respond, she hung up.

"Well?" Mike asked.

I looked at him and sighed. "I guess I'm going to New York."

God, let me get this right.

I didn't have much time to ponder the whirlwind of events. Within a matter of hours, I was on my way to New York. I threw a few things into my suitcase, and then Mike drove me to the airport.

As I settled into my seat on the plane, I closed my eyes, trying to rest for what was bound to be an emotionally and physically exhausting couple of days. But I was too wired to sleep—there was just so much to take in. In addition to appearing on *Good Morning America*, I would be on five other shows before the day's end.

My mind was racing. *I thought I'd stepped out of the limelight when I gave up modeling. How could one little blog post lead to all of this? Does the media want to hear about a Proverbs 31 wife? Do they even know what that means?*

I was used to media attention, but this was new territory. I opened my eyes and pulled out my Bible. Instead of sitting there worrying the entire flight, I figured I could get ready for the interviews by reading some of my favorite passages. I knew the stance I was taking in favor of modesty wouldn't be popular in certain circles—especially the modeling industry—and I wanted to make sure I was prepared. When my eyes skimmed over James 1:2-3, I couldn't help but smile: "Dear brothers and sisters, when troubles come your way, consider it an opportunity for great joy. For you know that when your faith is tested, your endurance has a chance to grow" (NLT).

Wow. How perfect is that? I thought. And suddenly it all started to make sense. The blog post, the media interest, the opportunity to share my story with the world. There was no question—God's fingerprints were all over this.

A quiet calm came over me as I leaned my head back and

silently prayed that God would shine through me during every interview. As I shared my story, I wanted to reflect His wisdom, His compassion, His humility, and His love. Modeling had been about bringing attention to myself, but now I prayed that the focus would be on God and the work He was doing inside me.

After several hours of praying and reading God's Word from my airplane-seat sanctuary, I closed my eyes, flooded with a sense of peace. I knew that God would watch over me through each of the interviews and that He would give me each word I needed to say.

When I arrived in New York, Sabrina met me with enough outfits to accommodate all of my interviews. After looking through everything she'd brought, I opted for a basic black, knee-length dress for the *GMA* piece. The dress was simple and understated, and it reflected my new standards for modesty. But truth be told, I was far less concerned about my appearance than I was with my message.

My entire worldview had changed radically over the past six months, and I desperately wanted my interviews to reflect that. I had taken a self-imposed hiatus from modeling so I could concentrate my time and energy on studying the Bible, attending our church in Montana, and learning my true identity—who God had made me to be. The Kylie Bisutti who was about to step in front of those television cameras was an entirely different person from the one millions of people had watched strut down the Victoria's Secret runway two years before.

The difference in my outward appearance would be easy to see. No more spray tan. No more highlights or dyed hair. No false eyelashes or heavy makeup. And a much healthier figure. But it was the changes that had taken place inside me—my commitment to Christ and to my husband, my deeper grasp on all God had done for me, and my understanding that true beauty comes from within—that I wanted viewers to see.

While getting my hair and makeup done, I could feel my heart pounding. I was nervous. Even more nervous than I'd been before I stepped on the Victoria's Secret runway for the first time. But this was different. This was important. I knew there were thousands of young girls out there who were trapped in the same debilitating cycle I'd struggled to break free from for years. The never-ending battle to be thin enough. Pretty enough. Perfect enough. I knew what it was like to constantly chase an ideal that's impossible to achieve—an ideal that's not even real to begin with. I had learned that the hard way. I hoped that by sharing my story, I could spare these girls some of the heartache and misery I'd experienced.

Just then, the stylist doing my hair leaned in and whispered, "We're all rooting for you." I looked up and noticed he had a Scripture verse tattooed on his forearm. We exchanged smiles, and my nervousness subsided a fraction.

Thank You, God, for small mercies.

The energy in the studio was electric, and my hands still were shaking a bit as I was led to my seat next to George Stephanopoulos. We exchanged a few pleasantries, and then he asked, "Are you ready?"

I took a deep breath. "Yes. I'm ready." And so it began.

George opened the interview by complimenting me, but I knew

what was coming. The questions were bound to get more difficult—and more pointed—as the interview progressed.

"Back in the Victoria's Secret model search in 2009, you were very determined to win," he said. "Here's what you said then: 'I have a very sweet personality, but don't let that fool you. I want this, and I'll do what it takes to get it.' So what changed?"

That's a fair question, I thought.

"Well, a lot," I answered aloud. "I was newly married at the time and growing in my relationship with the Lord. . . . I just became so convicted about wanting to honor my husband with my body and wanting to be a role model for other women out there who look up to me."

"Was there anything you learned from inside the business that turned you off? Or was that not really it?"

"It was really more of a heart issue for me." I tried to collect my thoughts and figure out how to expound on that in a way that would make my stance clearer, but before I could find the words, George continued.

"You had one encounter with a young cousin of yours that really made a difference," he said. "Tell us about that."

Perfect.

"Yes . . . I was doing my makeup in the mirror one day, and she was watching me. She was about eight at the time. I looked at her and said, 'Hey. What's going on?' She just looked at me and said, 'I think I want to stop eating so I can look like you.' It just broke my heart."

"And you realized that she wasn't alone, either," George said. "There are thousands of girls all across the country just like her."

I nodded. "Yes, thousands of girls who think that being beautiful is an outer issue when really it's a heart issue."

I wanted to continue on this topic, but George fired another question at me: "How did your husband handle all this? Did he have a problem with your modeling?"

"He was so supportive of me," I answered. "He obviously prayed about it, but I'm thankful he let me grow and come to this decision on my own."

"And when you came to it?" George asked with a wry smile.

"He was very thankful." I shared a laugh with George. "Very, very thankful."

"So what are you going to do now?" George continued. "You're not going to give up modeling completely."

"No, I'm definitely going to pursue modeling," I said. "I just want to be more wholesome about it. And the jobs that I choose are always going to be honoring the Lord."

And that was it.

The interview was over in less than three minutes. I was disappointed I hadn't been able to go into more depth, but given the time constraints, it was understandable. What was more disheartening for me, though, was that the entire time I was sharing my heart about modesty, the producers were running old video footage of me walking the Victoria's Secret runway in racy lingerie. As I was speaking about my desire to respect the Lord and my husband, they'd cut away to shots of me in skimpy bikinis looking anything but God-honoring. It was a complete disconnect from the life I was living now, and frankly, it was devastating.

Unfortunately, this part of my story was—and always will be—out of my control. Thanks to the Internet, all the inappropriate images that have been taken of me are out there, and as much as I'd love to, I can't flip a magic switch and make them go away.

But while it hurt to know that those images were flickering

across the screen behind me as I told about my journey, they also provided proof of the drastic change that had taken place in my life—the kind of change that only can happen as a result of God's grace.

I love the verse in Romans that says, "We know that in all things God works for the good of those who love him, who have been called according to his purpose." That footage is evidence that God can—and will—use even the most ungodly things for good.

In interview after interview that day, I shared my story and my faith. Of course, not every reporter was as fair and kind to me as George had been. Some tried to bait me into criticizing other models who were still in the industry, and others accused me of using my faith as some kind of marketing ploy to get some cheap PR. They offered me false praise for being a marketing genius, when in actuality nothing could have been further from the truth. I'd never seen any of this coming, and I was more shocked than anyone else that my decision had given me this opportunity to talk about my faith in front of a national audience.

Through it all, I leaned on God to keep me calm and focused, and I relied on the Bible to help me answer the tough questions. One of the verses I had memorized on the plane—"Blessed are those who are persecuted for righteousness' sake, for theirs is the kingdom of heaven" (Matthew 5:10, ESV)—was fresh in my mind, so whenever things became heated or difficult, I tried to just meditate on those words. True to His character, God saw me through.

After one of the last interviews of the afternoon, the female news anchor grabbed my hand and said, "I'm so thankful you're taking a stand, because I have a daughter who is caught up in all this body image stuff. It's about to destroy her."

This conversation was just one more confirmation that I was

doing the right thing. And although I was exhausted and hungry and more than ready to head home after almost ten hours of interviews, I felt peace about how the day had gone—even if there would be repercussions in the weeks ahead.

As soon as my plane touched down, I called Mike, who was still traveling on business, to tell him all about the interviews and the positive feedback I was receiving.

"It all makes sense to me now," I told him. "I think God allowed me to have this platform so I could share my story with other people. I was never meant to be a top model—I was meant to be a role model." I realized I was gushing, but I was so moved by everything that had happened that day.

I could almost hear Mike smiling through the phone. "God is amazing. And I'm so thankful for the work He's done in you." There was a pause, and I could tell Mike was choking back emotion. "This is an answer to my prayers," he said. "I'm so proud of you, honey."

As I settled into bed that evening, I tried to turn off my mind, but I couldn't. I couldn't stop thinking back over the past nine years—working in the modeling industry, becoming a Christian, marrying Mike, winning the Victoria's Secret contest. And through it all, God had been carefully guiding my every step—long before I was even aware of His presence. Now He was opening doors I never could have imagined.

The interviewers were right on one count—my story *was* the stuff of sheer genius. I just wasn't the genius behind it.

Chapter 2

JACKPOT

Don't be concerned about the outward beauty of fancy
hairstyles, expensive jewelry, or beautiful clothes.
You should clothe yourselves instead with the beauty
that comes from within, the unfading beauty of a
gentle and quiet spirit, which is so precious to God.

I PETER 3:3-4, NLT

PEOPLE OFTEN ASK ME how I got into modeling. Given my current
stance on modesty and the importance of inner beauty, diving into
a business that glorifies outward appearance and basically sells sex
doesn't seem like the most logical career choice. Looking back,
though, I can see that my journey has been a gradual one. God
has been leading me to the truth—one step at a time.

When I think about the beginning of my career path, I'm not
convinced I chose modeling so much as modeling chose me.

Growing up, I never was what you would call a "girly girl."
In fact, I was the complete opposite. I grew up in a little town
in northern Nevada called—of all things—Jackpot. Jackpot was
about seven hours by car from Las Vegas, but by virtually every
other standard, it was light-years away. We didn't have a movie

theater, a single clothing store, or even a fast-food restaurant. All we had was a general store, a gas station, a liquor store, a movie rental place, an old baseball field, and a handful of tiny casinos. It was a small town in every sense of the word.

Most of the people in Jackpot—my family included—were blue-collar workers, barely scraping together enough money to get by. We lived in a trailer until I was in first grade, and most of my clothes came from the thrift shop. By the world's standards, we unquestionably were poor. But as far as I was concerned, we had everything we needed and then some.

Neither of my parents had particularly glamorous jobs. Like most people in Jackpot, they worked at one of the local casinos. Mom had a job in housekeeping, and Dad was a poker dealer. They didn't make a lot of money, but there were intangible benefits that more than made up for the limited income. Mom worked mornings and afternoons, which meant she was home by the time I got back from school every day. And because Dad worked evenings, he also was home during the day. That gave us a lot of time to spend together as a family, and for us, that was far more important than money.

Family was—and still is—one of the most important parts of my life. And when I was growing up, I literally was surrounded by family.

My grandparents on my mom's side lived right next door, and all my cousins lived on our street too. There were nine of us kids, all around the same age, and we played together every day. A few nights a week, my entire family would eat dinner at Grandma and Grandpa's house. After dinner the adults would play pinochle while the cousins watched cartoons or played hide-and-seek outside. It was everything a kid could want.

While I loved spending time with my cousins, my grand-parents, and my mom, I especially adored the days I spent with my dad. Dad was a huge outdoorsman, whether he was hunting, fishing, camping, or riding ATVs. For the first ten years of my life, the two of us were inseparable. Every other weekend we'd go on some kind of outdoor adventure together—just the two of us. He taught me how to fish and hunt, and even how to dress a deer. I loved every minute of it. He was the center of my universe, and I would have done anything to make him happy.

I didn't realize how much I wanted to please my dad until the day of the ATV wreck. I was about eight years old, and I was rid-ing on the back of Dad's ATV, just as we'd done a thousand times before. But then some sagebrush caught my pant leg, pulling me off and under the ATV. Suddenly I felt a thousand pounds of pressure crushing my leg. It was excruciating. Dad had to back the four-wheeler off my leg to free me, and when he did, my body was racked with even more intense pain.

I could tell by the look on Dad's face that it was bad. He kept saying, "I'm so sorry, Ky Ky. I'm so sorry." There was no ques-tion—he was in as much pain emotionally as I was in physically. I'd never seen my dad so panic-stricken before, and observing him like that was almost more agonizing than my crushed leg.

Even at a young age, I sensed that the more upset I was, the more upset Dad would get. So I concentrated every bit of my energy on holding back my tears. I didn't make a sound as Dad drove me the thirty minutes back to where our truck was parked, another twenty-five minutes to Jackpot, and then forty-five more minutes to the hospital. I just bit my lip, swallowing the pain, and tried to focus on how Dad was holding up.

After we finally got to the ER, the doctor confirmed that I had a spiral fracture in my leg, meaning the bone had been twisted apart and the break wrapped all the way around my leg. Given the extent of the injury, the doctor was floored by how calm I was.

"You're a very brave little girl," he said to me.

I knew better. The reason I wasn't screaming and crying wasn't because of some superhuman courage; it was because I didn't want anyone to think my dad was a bad father—especially my dad.

When the doctor told me how brave I was, my dad's entire face lit up with pride. No matter what else happened that day, I had made my dad proud. And in my mind, that was the only thing that mattered.

My leg ended up healing beautifully, and I was only in a cast for about two months (although that felt like forever to my eight-year-old self). One thing was certain, though: the break didn't hinder my growth.

I wasn't particularly tall as a kid, but my legs were freakishly long compared to the rest of my body. In addition to my long legs, I was painfully thin, and the combination made me feel gangly and awkward. But while I was self-conscious about my body, the adults around me seemed to think I looked fabulous. Relatives, teachers—even strangers on the street—would tell me, "You really should be a model."

At first their comments struck me as strange, since I didn't put a lot of effort into the way I looked. I pretty much was a tomboy at heart, and most of my time was spent hunting and fishing and trudging through the woods with my dad. I was far more concerned with blending in with the sagebrush so I wouldn't frighten away the deer than I was with looking pretty.

Models stood out. I was more accustomed to blending in.

But the comments kept coming.

"You're so tall and thin—just like a model."

"What a pretty little girl. Have you ever thought about becoming a model?"

"Look at those long legs of yours. You could be a supermodel someday!"

In a way, being a model became my identity long before it ever became my career.

Adults don't always realize the profound effect their words can have on young kids—girls in particular. These people mean well, of course. What harm could possibly come from telling a little girl she's pretty? Technically, none—unless that's the only affirmation she ever hears. Unless that's the only reason she gets attention.

It wasn't as though I didn't have anything else going for me. I was a decent athlete—I especially loved to play basketball—and I quickly was becoming an excellent hunter. I also had a tender heart and cared about people who were hurting. Like all kids, I had praiseworthy qualities that extended beyond my appearance. But whenever anyone looked at me, all they seemed to see was *model*.

As my identity became wrapped up in being pretty, it also became the primary attribute I used to define my value. If people weren't praising me for my looks, I started feeling like I was lacking somehow, and I would go out of my way to make them like me. This would turn into a cycle that would haunt me for years to come.

No one in my family knew much about the modeling world, but my parents wanted to be supportive of me and whatever I wanted to do. So when I expressed an interest in modeling, my mom was willing to give it a try. The summer before I entered fourth grade, Mom heard about a casting call for young models in Twin Falls, Idaho. Since it was only about fifty miles away, she figured it would be a good place to start to see if modeling really was my thing.

Being new to all this, we weren't sure what everyone else would wear. I ended up in a blue denim dress we'd purchased at a local thrift store. It was used, but it still looked stylish.

When we arrived, we found out the casting agents were looking for school-age kids, both boys and girls, to accompany them to California in a few weeks to meet some of their biggest clients. I'd never been to a casting call before, so I wasn't sure what to expect. When they called my name, I walked and smiled and twirled for them, though I really had no idea what I was doing. But whatever I did must have worked, because they invited me to make the trip to California.

Mom and I were thrilled when they told us the news . . . until they told us the cost of the trip. It was way beyond our family budget, so my mom simply thanked them for the invitation, graciously explained that we couldn't afford it, and then we left.

Surprisingly, I wasn't that disappointed. I was hopeful that there would be other opportunities down the road. And I figured that if I really was meant to be a model, I'd get a second chance.

As it happened, we were about to move to a city where the very air was laced with hope and second chances.

Chapter 3

SIN CITY

For everything there is a season,
    a time for every activity under heaven. . . .
      A time to tear down and a time to build up.
    A time to cry and a time to laugh.
      A time to grieve and a time to dance.
ECCLESIASTES 3:1, 3-4, NLT

THEY SAY THAT ALL GOOD THINGS must come to an end, and unfortunately the idyllic childhood I had in Jackpot was no exception. One by one, my relatives started moving away. Work was hard to find in Jackpot, so they were forced to relocate to anywhere they could find jobs.

And then, just as I was getting ready to start fifth grade, Mom announced that we were moving out of Jackpot too.

I'd been raised not to whine or talk back, so I politely asked, "Where are we moving to?"

"About seven hours from here," she said. "To Las Vegas. Trust me, Kylie—you're going to love it."

I wasn't so sure I'd love it, but I was willing to give it a try. After all, we were going to be moving in with my mom's sister and her five children, which meant I'd have cousins to play with 24-7. Plus, I had a hunch that Vegas might be just the place to get my start in modeling.

Shortly after we arrived in Vegas, Mom took over as nanny for my five cousins, and Dad found a job in real estate. It didn't take long for me to admit that Mom was right: I did love it. In fact, in a lot of ways, life in Vegas wasn't all that different from what we'd left behind. I was surrounded by my cousins, Mom was home all the time, and even though Dad was now working days, he still carved out time to play hard-core Monopoly tournaments with my cousins and me and to watch movies with us in the evenings. I always chose the happily-ever-after movies, where the princess gets her happy ending. I might have been a tomboy, but I was a romantic at heart.

I started playing basketball at school and quickly found out I wasn't just a good player for Jackpot; I was good for Vegas. Of course, it didn't hurt that I kept getting taller. Mom, Dad, and my cousins came to cheer me on at every game, and I couldn't have been happier.

But between my sixth- and seventh-grade years, everything started to change. Dad was spending more and more time at work, and soon our movie nights and Monopoly tournaments went by the wayside. Worst of all, I sensed a growing disconnect between us. It felt like we were moving in opposite directions.

One morning I came up behind Dad while he was finishing the breakfast dishes and gave him a hug.

"Dad, I miss you," I said. "You've been working so much. I feel like I never see you anymore."

"I know, Ky." He dried his hands. "I'm working hard so you and your mom can have nice things. I want you to have what I didn't have growing up."

I didn't say anything, but deep down I missed our old life in Jackpot, when we had less money but more time together. Things were different now, and our lives were about to change even more.

Mom was expecting a baby in a few months, and I knew my new brother would take even more of my dad's attention away from me. I wasn't jealous. I just felt abandoned and confused. I might not have been able to put words to it then, but I knew I no longer was "Daddy's little girl." In fact, at thirteen years old and almost five feet eight inches tall, I wasn't a little girl anymore, period.

By the time I started eighth grade, I towered over most of the boys in my class. And I still was awkwardly thin. When you're in junior high, that's a perfect setup for getting teased. For a girl like me who tended to be on the sensitive side, it felt brutal. As I walked down the hall, girls I didn't even know would call me an "anorexic b----." These insults usually would be followed by laughter. The boys were slightly kinder to my face, calling me "giraffe." But both hurt.

As much as I told myself not to let the comments affect me, they did. For some reason, the boys' taunts bothered me even more than the girls' comments. I knew girls could be competitive and catty, but it cut deep to feel that kind of rejection from the boys.

Shortly after my brother, Luke, turned four months old, the four of us moved into our own house. I hoped that having our own place might bring Dad and me closer, but things just kept getting worse.

Dad was working all the time now, and even when he was home, he wasn't really present. His thoughts were constantly consumed by his job. We never went hunting anymore, and even when he took us to dinner or when we did something together as a family, he spent most of the time on his phone. I felt invisible.

Ironically, as Dad's attention waned, the attention I received from everyone else—including older boys—increased. Toward the end of my eighth-grade year, I started filling out in all the right places, and people began noticing me as something other than "giraffe."

That spring my mom sent pictures of me to various modeling companies in the area. The Envy Agency, one of the biggest modeling agencies in Las Vegas, expressed an interest and signed me to a contract. I was thrilled. Not only was this the second chance I'd been hoping for, but also I thought that if I could make it big as a model, it would prove something to all those people who had teased me at school. And on a deeper level, part of me dared to hope that this would help me regain my dad's attention somehow.

Everything's going to be different from now on, I promised myself.

I had no idea how prophetic that promise would be. But what never occurred to me at the time was that different doesn't always mean better.

I began modeling almost every weekend in style shows at the famous Fashion Show Mall in Vegas. At fourteen, I definitely was one of the younger models with my agency, so they started building my portfolio with pictures that made me look older. They coated my face with makeup, giving my eyes a sultry, smoky look. I spent hours with a stylist until they were satisfied with my big, "sexy" hair. Finally, they dressed me in revealing clothes that would have been risqué for someone of any age, let alone a girl barely out of junior high.

I didn't understand it at the time, but ultimately the modeling industry's job is to sell sex. Even ads aimed at women featuring women tend to have a sexy edge to them, especially when it comes to fashion. Revealing outfits, provocative poses, seductive looks— it's all part of the package. They're selling the idea that men want to be with the models they see in those ads, and as a result, women want to *be* those models. The designers know it. The advertisers know it. The photographers know it.

It wouldn't be long before I knew it too.

I'll never forget my first photo shoot for Envy.

The photographer kept pushing me to strike more and more provocative poses. It didn't matter to him that I'd just turned fourteen—in fact, I doubt he even knew how old I was. Between the hair, the makeup, and the outfit, I easily could have passed for eighteen—possibly even twenty. And that was how the industry worked: for all practical purposes, I was a mannequin the photographer could pose and contort however he wanted. In modeling, it's not about the person in the image; it's all about the image. The photographer wanted the perfect shot. And, anxious to please and to be accepted, I wanted to do everything just right.

The more the photographer encouraged me to play to the camera, the more I worked it. And I was surprisingly good at it.

As much as I regret it now, at the time I didn't feel guilty about striking those provocative poses. I just saw it as part of the job. I heard the photographer tell me, "You're so sexy. You're so gorgeous," enough times that eventually I started to believe him. After all the teasing I'd endured at school, it felt good to have someone compliment me on my looks. The more positive feedback I got, the more willing I was to push the envelope and make him happy. It was the beginning of a cycle that would end up consuming my life.

But for someone who wanted to get experience in the modeling world, the Fashion Show Mall was the ideal setting. I learned how to walk a runway, how to play to a crowd, and how to turn and move in a way that showed off the best features of a wide variety of clothes.

I also learned how to do wardrobe changes quickly. At the Mall the runway came up from underground, and the only place available to change was a small, boxed-in area with transparent walls—meaning no privacy. I didn't even like changing into my PE clothes in the school locker room, and now I was expected to strip down in front of not only the other models, but the male security guards as well.

I quickly discovered that if I was going to make it as a model, I'd need to get over my shyness because there was no room for modesty or propriety backstage at a fashion show. This was new, uncomfortable territory for me, but I figured I had no other choice. At the time I didn't have the perspective to understand that some things just aren't worth compromising on.

It was my start down a very slippery slope.

Chapter 4

BANGKOK OR BUST

Let no one deceive you with empty words.

EPHESIANS 5:6

"THAILAND?" I asked Daniel, my agent. I glanced at my mom in disbelief, but she didn't say a word.

"Yes, Thailand," he continued. "It's just for the summer. You'll mostly be modeling formal wear, and it's a great way for young models like you to get some experience under your belt."

I just sat there, mute, so Daniel went on. "Clients like to see that you've worked overseas. It shows diversity." He paused and looked right at me. "So, what do you think?"

I had no idea *what* to think. I liked the idea of getting more experience and building my portfolio. But Thailand? I'd never even been outside of the States.

"We'll talk about it," Mom answered, smiling at me.

After we got home, Mom and Dad stayed up late into the night talking. I was in my room, but I could hear snippets of their conversation. I could tell there were things about the trip that made them a little uneasy. It was a long way from home. And I was very young—only fourteen. But they both knew how much modeling meant to me, and they wanted to do whatever they could to help me achieve my dreams. And they figured that since it was a summer job, it wouldn't interfere with school.

The next morning they announced their decision: I could go, on one condition. Mom would be going with me, at least for a few weeks, until I got settled. A relieved grin stretched across my face. To me it was the best possible scenario—not only would I get to experience this once-in-a-lifetime opportunity, but I wouldn't have to do it alone.

Once we landed in Thailand, I realized just how grateful I was to have Mom with me. Neither one of us had ever been out of the country before, and we didn't know anyone there. To make things more challenging, we also were up against quite a language barrier. When we stepped off the plane, all we had was an address for the apartment we would be staying in, our luggage, and each other.

Once outside the airport, we hopped into the first available taxi, and Mom handed our driver the address. He spoke very little English, but he seemed to understand where we wanted to go. Eventually, after navigating the crowded streets of downtown Bangkok, we ended up at the apartment complex. The apartment the agency had arranged for us to stay in was nothing fancy, but it was clean, and there was plenty of room for Mom and me to spread out.

After we unpacked, we met several of the other models who

were staying at the same complex. A few of them were from the United States, and two were from Europe. All the girls had been there for several weeks already, so they filled us in on everything we needed to know, like how to get to and from casting calls, where we could go shopping, and how to get around without knowing the language. I was relieved to find out that at least the booking agents spoke English.

The next day we went to the agency headquarters in downtown Bangkok, where I was immediately whisked away to hair and makeup. I had what they called "virgin hair," meaning it never had been colored, highlighted, or permed. For some reason unbeknownst to me, they insisted on dying it black. Jet black. When I saw my reflection in the mirror, I barely recognized myself. I thought the coloring made me look really pale, but that was the look they were going for, apparently. I had no choice but to go along with it. And I knew it could have been worse.

Back in Vegas, I'd seen models go through some pretty drastic styling. I remember one girl who broke down sobbing after they completely hacked off her bangs—with no warning at all. Not only did it look terrible, but since they lopped off more than ten inches, it also was going to take forever to grow back. The stylist barely noticed. He'd gotten the look he wanted for that particular shot, and that was all that mattered.

That's one of the harsh realities I learned early on about the modeling industry: ultimately, your body doesn't really belong to you. It belongs to the client. Since they're paying, they figure they can do pretty much whatever they want to you. They can curl your hair, straighten it, dye it, cut it—even shave it. I've seen hair extensions being pulled out by the roots and smoke billowing out of flat irons while the hair inside got singed and fried. I've watched models squeeze into shoes so small their feet literally bled, and I've seen false eyelashes torn off so quickly that the natural lashes came off with them. Modeling may look glamorous on the outside, but believe me, beauty can be an ugly business.

I had a casting call immediately following my dye job, so Mom and I took the map the agency had given us and navigated our way to the client's office. Bangkok has kind of a street-fair atmosphere both day and night, so not only did we have to figure out where we were going, but we also had to weave in and out of the hundreds of people who filled the sidewalks and spilled onto the streets. And since few people spoke English, it was nearly impossible to communicate or ask for help with directions.

As we walked through the city, the stench was overwhelming. We never figured out what smelled so bad, but we suspected it had something to do with the hundreds of dogs roaming the streets. It seemed there were three dogs to every person in Bangkok, and the streets were overcrowded as it was. On top of everything else, it was unbelievably hot—even for a girl who had grown up in the desert—making for a sticky, chaotic adventure every time we left the apartment. I'd never felt so far from home in my life.

Mom went with me to each casting call after that, and I was glad. I couldn't imagine being there alone. In addition to the dogs, there were also sleazy characters lurking in the streets who scoured the city for girls to lure into the sex trade. From the research we'd done prior to the trip, Mom and I knew that sex trafficking was a prevalent problem in Thailand. But reading about it is one thing; seeing it happen right in front of you is another.

One afternoon, as Mom and I were fighting our way through the crowded streets en route to yet another casting call, the nonstop schedule, the extreme heat, and an empty stomach finally caught up with me. The next thing I knew, I was lying on the sidewalk. I had collapsed from a combination of heat exhaustion and hypoglycemia. Thank God Mom was with me, or who knows what could have happened.

Mom helped me to my feet and, after making sure I wasn't injured, started looking for a place where we could sit down and get something to eat. It was hard to find American food in Bangkok, but a few days earlier, Mom had managed to track down a Pizza Hut on the other side of the city. We hadn't even been in Thailand for two weeks, and I was already desperate for American food. I couldn't wait to sink my teeth into a piece of pepperoni deep dish. It seemed like the perfect cure for what was ailing me— the hypoglycemia *and* the homesickness.

The harsh reality was that it was just about time for Mom to head back home. With one-year-old Luke at home, she needed to get back to him and the rest of the family.

As we waited for our pizza, Mom expressed her concerns about leaving me. "Ky, what if you pass out again and I'm not here to help you?" she asked. "You're only fourteen, and you're basically on your own here. I know we agreed to give this a shot, but now I'm not so sure."

I was only half-listening to Mom because I was distracted by a seedy-looking man at a nearby table, talking to two girls who didn't look like they originally were from Thailand. They looked about my age, probably fourteen or fifteen, and from what I could make out, he was trying to coax them into working for him.

"You're both so beautiful," he told them. "You stand out in the crowd."

I could see the girls' faces light up with every flattering remark.

Modeling is a desperate business, and a little flattery can go a long way. It was obvious this guy knew what he was doing, and those girls were naively playing right into his hands. He made lots of promises and was doing his best to sound genuine, but I just didn't trust him. I felt so scared for the two girls. And I felt scared for myself.

How am I going to survive here without my mom?

By now Mom had started watching the horrific little scene playing out at the table a few feet away. And she had seen enough. "That's it, Ky," she said firmly. "You're coming home with me."

I let out a huge sigh. *Thank goodness,* I thought. As much as I wanted to build my portfolio, at that moment all I wanted was to go home.

We went back to the apartment, packed our bags, and headed to the agency to break the news. Mom thanked them for the opportunity and explained that I wasn't feeling well enough to continue in Bangkok that summer. The booking agents weren't pleased with our decision, but they didn't try to stop us. Not that it would have made a difference if they had. There was no way Mom was going to leave her baby girl in Bangkok without adult supervision.

On the plane ride home, I thought about those girls at Pizza Hut. I hoped they were okay. I also thought about my modeling opportunities and hoped I wouldn't be in too much trouble at Envy for bailing after only two weeks. I thought about my little brother and my dad, and how much I couldn't wait to see them.

I also thought about my hair, and how I was definitely dying it back to brown the moment we landed in Vegas.

As expected, Envy was appalled that I'd walked away from the Bangkok opportunity after only two weeks, but no one dwelled on the matter long. Truth be told, I was too valuable for them to stay mad at me. Between the Fashion Show Mall gigs and the smattering of print jobs I'd done in and around Vegas, I was making decent money—and they were getting 20 percent of everything I made. Plus, at fourteen, I still had at least four or five good years left in me. No point in leaving money on the table.

"Maybe you can try Thailand again in a few years," my agent said.

And that was the end of it.

With brown hair once again, I soon was back at the Fashion Show Mall doing six runway shows a day almost every weekend. Since there only were nine of us working the shows, I got to know the other models pretty well and even became close to some of them. I didn't know it at the time, but this is pretty rare, since the constant competition and high turnover rate tend to prevent friendships from forming among fellow models.

I especially bonded with a girl named Asia. Like me, Asia was a little curvier than your typical model. And when I say *curvy*, what I really mean is that we both had hips. Not big hips, mind you— just hips. In the modeling world, anything over thirty inches is considered curvy, and curvy does not play well on the runway— especially in high fashion, where being rail thin is considered the ideal. Horrifying as it may sound, some models even go so far as to have their hip bones surgically shaved down to reach that precious thirty-inch mark. Others have their bottom ribs removed so they look ultra-thin. It just felt like part of the industry to me when I was starting out, but now it breaks my heart to think of girls and young women using surgery to deform the beautiful way God created them.

With hips measuring roughly thirty-six inches, I was practically obese by modeling standards. But there was one place where being curvy did play well: Victoria's Secret.

Though extremely well toned and thin, Victoria's Secret models tend to be shapelier than your typical runway model. Runway models are built straight up and down so the clothes fall on them like they're on hangers. If you've ever watched a high-end fashion show, you know that the edge goes to models who are thin to the point of being gaunt.

But lingerie—especially Victoria's Secret lingerie—is designed to give women *more* curves than they have naturally. I remember the first time my mom and I went into a Victoria's Secret store at the mall in Vegas. The walls were covered with enormous pictures of the most beautiful women I had ever seen. Victoria's Secret's elite models are called Angels, and to me, that's exactly what they appeared to be. Everything about them seemed perfect—their hair, their skin, their bodies. Like me, they were lanky yet curvy; unlike me, they all seemed confident, outgoing, and bubbly. They were the embodiment of everything the world deemed sexy and desirable, and like millions of girls all over the world, I wanted to be just like them.

Both my friend Asia and I had fallen under the Angels' spell. We were among the millions who tuned in every December to watch the sexiest women on earth strut their stuff on the runway in the most lavish and spectacular fashion show of the year. During breaks between our own fashion shows, we would take to the empty runway and practice *the walk*. Here's the thing: Angels don't just walk the runway; they work it. They work their hips, and they work the crowd. Angels are put on the runway with one intention: to seduce every man within eyeshot. It would be years before the Lord would awaken me to the twisted irony in that:

angels, depicted in the Bible to be God's messengers, being portrayed as sex symbols.

But for now, all Asia and I could see was the perceived glamour of it all. Between shows we'd put on the tightest, most revealing outfits we could find and strut our stuff on the Fashion Show Mall runway, throwing out our hips, striking provocative poses, winking, blowing kisses, and flirting with our imaginary admirers. Every so often, we'd catch the attention of men walking by, and they'd stop and flirt with us, telling us how gorgeous we were and feeding our egos. The fact that we weren't even sixteen didn't matter to the grown men who gawked and whistled and made suggestive comments to us.

"Someday we're going to be Victoria's Secret Angels," Asia would whisper to me in a low, conspiratorial voice.

"You know it," I'd whisper back, shooting her a sly grin.

For the most part, we were just joking around and having fun. But deep down, both of us desperately longed for the glamorous life we imagined Victoria's Secret Angels led—the attention, the fashion, the fame. I had no idea yet how empty and unsatisfying that lifestyle could be. As teenage girls, we simply were enamored with the aura of being an Angel. And in the modeling world, it doesn't get any bigger than that.

Chapter 5

FIRSTS

Wisdom will save you from the ways of wicked men,
from men whose words are perverse.

PROVERBS 2:12

WHEN I STARTED high school that fall, I was five feet nine and growing up fast—too fast. Practically overnight, it seemed, I was starting to attract the attention of a lot of junior and senior guys. And although part of me secretly enjoyed this kind of attention, I wasn't mature enough to handle it. I was a little girl in a woman's body, which can be a dangerous combination.

That fall I met Jake. On the surface, Jake was everything a girl could want. Not only was he a senior, but he also was the star of the football team. He was popular, confident, outgoing, and yes, attractive. What I didn't know at the time was that he also had a reputation at school for being a shameless player.

From the moment Jake and I met, he said and did all the right things. He showered me with gifts and compliments and made me feel like I was the most beautiful girl in the world. With each day that passed, each phone call filled with promises and words of affirmation, each token of affection, Jake fed into my insecurities and my desire to be loved and accepted. It wasn't long before I was so taken in that I would have done almost anything to make him happy—even if it meant deceiving my parents or, for that matter, myself.

Now, my parents had made it abundantly clear that I wasn't allowed to date until I was sixteen, and when I was growing up, my parents' word was pretty much law. I never talked back, I never argued with them, I never kept secrets from them, and it never would have occurred to me to go behind their backs or against their wishes.

All of that was about to change.

It started with homecoming. After a few weeks of casual flirting at school, Jake asked me if I'd be his date for the homecoming dance. I liked Jake, and I was flattered by the offer, but I knew my parents were firm in their stance. Jake, however, wouldn't take no for an answer. And since I didn't want to risk losing him, I begged my parents to make an exception this one time. I mounted a flimsy argument that it wasn't really a date (although obviously it was)—it was just a school function (which happened to involve a limo and reservations at a restaurant nowhere near the school).

At first, my parents stood firm. They still felt I was too young to date, and the fact that Jake was three years older than me didn't exactly help my cause. Looking back, I guess my first clue that Jake was bad news should have been the fact that he never offered to speak to my parents himself. He just guilt-tripped me into doing his dirty work for him.

Eventually, after days of begging and pleading, I convinced

my parents to let me go. They reluctantly agreed—on one condition: we were not to go anywhere near the infamous Vegas Strip. I shared this stipulation with Jake, who coolly assured me that our evening would not involve the Strip in any way. And being naive, I believed him.

When homecoming arrived, Jake came to my house to meet my parents and take a few pictures. Dad was at work, but Mom was there to greet him. Jake was almost painfully polite as he assured my mom that we weren't going anywhere near the Strip and promised that he'd have me home at a decent hour. Jake wasn't just smooth with the young ladies; he knew how to work the mothers, too.

After posing for a few pictures, we said good-bye to my mom and headed for the car. Jake opened my car door and helped me in. Then he walked over to the driver's side and got in, but instead of starting the car, he just stared at me.

"What?" I asked.

"I just want to look at you," he said. "You're so beautiful, baby. I'm the luckiest guy in the world."

I was officially hooked.

A few minutes later, we pulled into a parking lot, where Jake had promised a limo would be waiting to take us to Black Angus for dinner. But instead of a limousine, there was a party bus—and about four other couples, all seniors, milling around taking pictures.

Sensing my confusion, Jake blurted out, "What is this? We were supposed to have a limo!" He made his way over to one of the guys in the group, and the two of them appeared to have a heated conversation.

Jake claimed he had no idea the limo had been swapped out at the last minute for a party bus, and at the time I believed him.

But knowing what I know now, I have a feeling he knew exactly what would be going down that night.

For a moment I considered calling my mom to let her know we were going to be riding in a party bus instead of a limousine. But given how reluctant she'd been to let me go in the first place, I was afraid that if I spilled it now, she'd pull the plug on the whole evening. And that would have sunk me with Jake for sure. So I rationalized that a party bus wasn't really *that* different from a limo, kept my mouth shut, and went along with it.

As soon as the bus started, the party started. Music blared, and everyone got up to dirty dance in the aisle. Well, almost everyone. I was too stunned to move. This was not what I'd expected. And it certainly wasn't what Jake had promised the evening would be like. I sensed that Jake wanted to get up and join the dancing, but my body language made it pretty clear I was not comfortable, so he just sat next to me and watched the other couples. Now my discomfort was coupled with guilt. Guilt over ruining Jake's senior homecoming. Guilt over not coming clean with Mom about the party bus. And this party was just getting started.

At the dance, there was more picture taking, more dancing. Even though I was the only freshman in our group and felt distinctly out of place with everyone else, I was strangely at ease with Jake. The way he heaped on the flattery and charm, it was hard not to be. He told me I was beautiful and sexy. And that was exactly what my fragile self-image craved.

After the dance, I assumed we were getting back on the bus and heading to Black Angus for dinner. After all, that's what Jake had told me, and that's what he'd confirmed with my mom. I was so distracted by the other couples making out around us that it took me a while to realize we were going the wrong way.

After a few minutes, my uneasiness got the better of me, and I asked if we were getting close to Black Angus.

"We're not going to Black Angus." One of Jake's friends came up for air just long enough to answer my question. "We can find something to eat on the Strip."

I panicked. I would be grounded for life if we went to the Strip.

"I can't go to the Strip," I whispered to Jake. "You know what my parents said."

"I don't know what to do, baby," Jake replied with a shrug. "My friends changed the plans. I had nothing to do with it."

At this point I figured I had two options—I could get grounded now, or I could get grounded later. I figured the sooner I called my mom, the better.

Maybe she won't be as mad if I call her as soon as we get to the Strip and let her know what happened.

I was wrong. She was livid. Even worse in my mind, she was disappointed. She said I should have called her when I first found out we were going in a party bus and not a standard limo, like we'd promised.

"I'm on my way to pick you up," she said.

I'd never been in this much trouble in my life.

When my mom pulled up in front of the restaurant on the Strip, Jake hung back with his friends and let me take all the heat. As I crawled into her car, he barely made eye contact with me.

"I am very disappointed in you, Kylie." Mom sat in the driver's seat, staring straight ahead.

"I know." I sighed. "I'm sorry."

And I was. I'd never deceived my mom like this before. It felt terrible.

Yet as bad as I felt about disappointing my mom, I felt even worse about letting Jake down. He was my first boyfriend, and I had completely ruined our first real date. I now know that the Bible offers plenty of warnings not to fall prey to people like this— people who lead you down a path of lies and destruction—but at the time I still was under Jake's spell.

He's going to hate me now, I thought as Mom pulled into our driveway. *How can I ever face him again?*

My thoughts were interrupted by Mom's voice.

"Go to bed," she ordered. "We'll discuss this in the morning."

Feeling utterly defeated and exhausted, I simply nodded and retreated to my room.

I plopped down on my bed and kicked off my shoes. *Jake is never going to talk to me again,* I thought. Just moments later, my cell phone rang.

Apparently, I was wrong.

Jake and I talked several more times that week—both on the phone and at school. My mom and I talked a lot that week too. About Jake. About my life. And about my future.

"Kylie, the reason your dad and I are so strict with you is because we want the best for you," Mom began. "And boys Jake's age are all alike. They're only after one thing. And as soon as you give it up, they'll be done with you."

"I know, Mom." I shifted uncomfortably in my chair. "I understand. Really." The truth was, I didn't. I just wanted the conversation to end. But Mom wasn't finished.

"Just save yourself for marriage, honey," she continued. "It will be so much more special if you do."

"I will. I promise."

I didn't realize it at that moment, but I had just lied to my mom. Again.

True to their word, my parents remained unmovable about their no-dating-before-sixteen restriction. So, in line with what quickly was becoming a habit for me, I rationalized a way around the rule.

They did forbid me to date, I reasoned, but they didn't say anything about having an at-school boyfriend. Just like that, I had a loophole.

That's the thing about deception. Once you start, it's hard to stop. And it can snowball on you very quickly, until things are completely out of control. In just a few weeks' time, I had become frighteningly adept at shading the truth to get my way. And I was about to pay for it—big-time.

During school hours, Jake and I were officially an item, and everyone—with the exception of my parents—knew it. He wrote me love letters and left them in my locker; we held hands in the school hallways; he played me romantic songs over the phone and told me that each one reminded him of me. I loved every minute of it. Mom didn't like the amount of time I spent talking to Jake in the evenings, and she even threatened to take away my phone if I didn't scale it back. I promised her I would. But I didn't. Dad was still working extremely long hours; Mom was busy taking care of Luke and keeping things running at home; and frankly it gave me a thrill to spend my evenings on the phone with someone who wanted to talk to me more than anyone else in the world.

After a while, though, just talking on the phone wasn't enough. Although I couldn't go on official dates with Jake, we found ways to get together outside the school walls. We would arrange to "accidentally" bump into each other with our friends at the movies, or we'd "just happen" to show up at the same restaurant at the same time on weekends. My parents were oblivious to it all.

In retrospect, the fact that I felt the need to hide my relationship with Jake from my parents should have been a glaring warning sign that what I was doing was wrong. But I was so consumed with the attention I was getting from Jake that I became blind to everything else.

Right before Christmas, I went to the mall with my two best friends, and Jake met us there. It was the last time I'd see him before my family and I traveled to Utah for the remainder of Christmas break. Jake surprised me by taking me to Build-A-Bear. We walked through the store hand in hand and chose matching teddy bears to build. Then we selected the hearts that would go inside each bear—he kissed my bear's heart, and I kissed his. As cheesy as it sounds now, at the time I felt like a princess in a fairy tale, being wooed and courted. *So this is what it's like to be adored,* I thought.

"I'll miss you," I said, hugging him one last time.

"I'll miss you, too," he said. Then he whispered in my ear, "I love you."

I froze. It was the first time he'd said that to me. In fact, it was the first time anyone outside my family had ever said those words to me—and it caught me completely off guard. Two minutes ago, we'd been playing with teddy bears like a couple of little kids, and now this? I honestly didn't know how I felt about Jake, but I was pretty sure I didn't love him. No, I was sure I didn't—at least not yet. I was also sure of something else. When someone says, "I love you," they expect to hear it back. That's when panic set in. *Everything has been so perfect. What if I don't say it back? Will he break up with me?*

And without even thinking, I heard myself say, "I love you, too." I was struck by how strange the words sounded coming out of my mouth. With my family, they felt natural, right. But with Jake . . .

"See you when I get back," I blurted out, pulling myself free from his embrace, suddenly anxious to get as far away from him as possible. No. I definitely didn't love him.

What I didn't realize, though, was that his words were just part of his game. He didn't love me, either.

⚜

That spring I decided to go out for track—in part because I genuinely enjoyed sports, but mostly because Jake ran track too, and I jumped at every opportunity to spend more time with the guy who had become my whole world.

Surprisingly, when I told Jake about my decision to join the team, he wasn't as excited as I thought he'd be. He even seemed a little upset about it. I couldn't make sense of it . . . until a few weeks into practice.

Her name was Jessica. She was an upperclassman, and Jake seemed to spend an inordinate amount of time flirting with her—both during and after practice. In fact, rumors had begun circulating that Jake had taken Jessica to a couple of parties. I was devastated, but what could I do? I still wasn't allowed to date Jake officially, which meant I wasn't able to go to parties with him on the weekends. So he could get together with anyone he wanted to outside of school, and I wouldn't even know about it. It was a great setup for Jake. But it was a lousy one for me.

I was starting to get panicky. I was willing to do anything so I wouldn't lose him. And Jake knew it.

He began saying things like, "We've been dating for a long time now, and I want you to be my first. I love you." All his friends and their girlfriends were having sex, a fact that Jake pointed out to me on a regular basis. I held my ground, though. I wanted to save myself for my husband. But I was starting to get a sinking feeling that Jake was losing interest in me.

Our nightly phone calls started to taper off, and when he did call, we didn't talk for hours like we once had. And then there were the rumors about Jessica. Inwardly, I was starting to spiral out of control. The thought of losing Jake's attention was almost more than I could bear. I was terrified, desperate, and lost. That's when he played his final hand.

One afternoon before lunch, Jake met me at my locker and began quoting lines from my favorite movie, *The Notebook*. Then he grabbed my hand, smiled at me, and whispered, "Let's blow off lunch and go for a little ride."

It had been a while since Jake had sought me out at school, so even though I really didn't like to leave campus during the day, I agreed. How I didn't see what was coming next still is beyond me.

We got in Jake's car, and he popped in a CD he'd made that featured all my favorite love songs. It was a beautiful March day. The sun was shining, and the breeze was blowing in my hair. There I was, out with my favorite person. For the first time in weeks, everything seemed perfect again. Then Jake stopped the car, unfastened his seat belt, and reached over to caress my face and brush the hair from my eyes.

"I don't want to pressure you, baby, but I really want you to be my first," he whispered. "I love you so much." Then he ran his hand up my skirt.

My mind went blank. My body became numb. I knew what was happening, and I knew I wasn't ready for it, but at that moment, I felt paralyzed. And utterly powerless to stop it.

It was over as quickly as it had begun, and before I could even begin to process what had just happened, we were headed back to school for our afternoon classes.

I climbed out of the car like a zombie, gazing blankly around the parking lot. Nothing seemed real. It was as if the last half hour had all been a dream. No—a nightmare.

Jake quickly kissed me on the cheek and said, "Bye, babe." Then he left me standing there and headed off to class.

In my head, all I could hear were my mother's words playing over and over again on a loop: *Boys Jake's age are all alike. They're only after one thing. And as soon as you give it up, they'll be done with you.*

But I'd been so sure Jake was different. He had been patient with me. He waited two full months before he kissed me. He even told me he wanted to marry me after we graduated. And he'd told me countless times that he loved me.

How had I missed the truth?

Two weeks later I started hearing more rumors about Jake and Jessica—this time that they'd had sex. When I confronted Jake about it, he blew up at me. He told me to stop acting jealous, and he accused me of being paranoid. In the end, he did just about everything he could to shift the blame onto me. But he never actually came out and denied it.

After that, Jake seemed to turn into someone else. He was distant at school. He stopped calling. And then one day between classes, he pulled me aside in the stairwell and said those infamous words: "We need to talk."

"This just isn't working for me anymore." His face was blank, and there was virtually no emotion in his voice. "I mean, your parents won't even allow you to go on dates with me."

Deep down, I'd known something like this was coming. But hearing him say the words out loud terrified me.

"You knew that when we first started seeing each other," I pleaded. "What about all those hours we spent on the phone and all the times we spent together at the mall? Didn't those things mean anything to you?" I could feel tears stinging my eyes.

"Yeah, I guess." He shrugged his shoulders nonchalantly. "But this just isn't working for me anymore, you know?"

No. I didn't.

"Please don't break up with me." Tears were starting to brim over. Then things turned ugly.

"Do you want me to quit track? I will." I was begging now. "And I'll talk to my parents again about going out with you. Please, just don't do this to us, Jake."

I gasped for breath between my tears. "I'm sorry I accused you of cheating on me. I'll change. I'll do whatever you want to make this right. Just don't break up with me. Please! I'll do anything!"

He was unmovable. "It's just not going to work." He kissed my forehead. "Sorry, babe." And with that, he walked out of the stairwell.

I collapsed right there on the stairs, crying uncontrollably.

Mom was right. She was so right. At that moment, all I wanted to do was run into my mom's arms, pour my heart out to her, and have her hold me until the pain went away. But there was no way I could do that. I'd been lying to my parents for the past six months about seeing Jake. How could I possibly tell them about this? All my sneaking around had finally caught up with me. Now here I was, huddled in the stairway, devastated and frightened. And utterly alone.

Days turned into weeks without a single phone call from Jake.

I knew it was over. I'd been played—from the very beginning. And because I'd been so desperate to hold on to him, I'd gone along with it all, ignoring every red flag along the way.

As I reflect on all the missteps I made and the deceptions I believed leading up to that nightmare, I'd give almost anything to go back and undo what happened. But I've learned that God has a way of using even our most horrific moments and our worst mistakes for good. I'm not proud of the decisions I made during my relationship with Jake. But the Lord used those decisions and the pain they caused to lead me to the best thing that ever happened to me.

Chapter 6

A SECOND CHANCE

GOD, my God, I yelled for help
and you put me together.
GOD, you pulled me out of the grave,
gave me another chance at life
when I was down-and-out.

PSALM 30:2-3, *The Message*

THE NEXT FEW WEEKS made my breakdown in the stairwell look like a picnic. Every day I came home right after track practice, went to my room, and sobbed. The fact that I couldn't talk to my parents about what had happened made me feel even worse. I knew they loved me, but I just couldn't bring myself to tell them—or anyone else, for that matter—what I'd done. I felt used and stupid and embarrassed and hurt all at the same time. I didn't care about anything anymore—not my schoolwork, not track, not modeling, not my relationships with the people I loved. I was desperate and depressed, and I was spiraling downward in a hurry.

Even my dad, who barely seemed to notice me at all anymore, could tell something was wrong.

"Hey, Kylie." He stopped me one evening as I breezed past him on my way to my room. "What's wrong with you lately? Why have you been acting so sad?"

I didn't know what to say. I didn't want to lie to him, but I knew I never could tell him the truth.

"I don't want to talk about it," I said quietly.

. "Are you sure?" He looked at me closely, concern etched on his face. "You know you can tell me anything, Kylie."

Ouch. Yes, there had been a time when I could have told my dad anything. But those days were long gone. Besides, how could I possibly tell him about this? It wasn't like I'd spilled soda on the rug or scratched the door of his car with my bike. Mistakes like those could be fixed easily. What I had done with Jake was—in my mind, at least—unforgivable.

It wasn't just my dad who seemed far away now. As much as I adored my little brother, I wasn't spending time with him, either. I wanted to be alone all the time. Mom still was taking me to modeling auditions, but I didn't really care if I got the jobs or not. As we were leaving one audition, we passed a wishing well. Mom asked Luke if he wanted a penny so he could make a wish, and he nodded his head excitedly. After he threw the penny into the water, Mom asked him what he'd wished for.

"I wished that Kylie would be happy again." He looked up at me, flashing his most hopeful smile.

Normally that would have broken my heart. But my heart already was broken. Frankly, I couldn't muster the emotion to care about anything. And I certainly couldn't imagine ever being happy again.

I tried my best to put on a brave face at school, but I wasn't fooling anyone. It was obvious to everyone—even those who didn't know me—that I was a mess. For the most part, people kept their distance. Then one day in weight-training class, a girl I'd never spoken to before approached me and asked if I'd be interested in attending her church's youth group with her that week.

Her name was Catalina. She seemed nice enough, but I really didn't know her. I think I was even more surprised than she was when I heard myself say, "Sure. When is it?"

"It's on Wednesday night at seven." She grabbed a piece of paper, scribbled a note on it, and handed it to me.

"Here's the address," she said with a genuine smile. "I really hope you'll come."

And then something even more unexpected happened. For the first time in weeks, I felt a smile creep across my face.

On Wednesday, when Mom pulled up to the address Catalina had written down, I was surprised to find that it wasn't a church; it was someone's house. I breathed a sigh of relief. My family didn't attend church, and the idea made me a little uncomfortable. The fact that Catalina's youth group met at a house somehow helped take the edge off.

"I'll call you when I'm ready to come home, okay?" I said to Mom as I climbed out of the car.

"Okay, honey. And, Kylie, try to have a good time, okay?" Poor Mom. The past few weeks hadn't been particularly easy on her, either.

I nodded and smiled, trying to appear as upbeat as possible. The prospect of having a good time seemed highly unlikely, and yet for some reason, as I started walking toward the house, I felt strangely optimistic.

I took a deep breath and rang the doorbell, unsure of what to expect. I half imagined a classroom-like setting, with a teacher up front lecturing while everyone took notes, so I was shocked to open the door and find a party going on inside. Everywhere I looked, groups of kids were talking, laughing, and eating, and a few guys were throwing around a football out back. As I made my way through the room, people would stop their conversations to smile at me and say hello. It was strange—for the past month and a half, every time I walked down the hallway at school, people I'd known for years either would give me looks of disgust or ignore me altogether, lest they be sucked into my vortex of misery and despair. But here, total strangers seemed genuinely happy to see me.

I was looking around the room, trying to take it all in, when I heard a familiar voice call out, "Kylie! Over here." There was Catalina, standing with a group of about five or six girls, smiling and waving me over. When I finally made it across the crowded room, she hugged me, thanked me for coming, and started introducing me to everyone. It turned out that most of the people in Catalina's youth group went to a different high school.

Well, that explains it, I thought. With the exception of one or two close friends, most of the people at my school treated me like I had some horribly contagious disease. But already I could tell these people were different. They really seemed interested in getting to know me as a person. None of them commented on my height or my figure. And not one of them knew about my disastrous relationship with Jake.

After a little more socializing, we broke up into smaller groups and began talking about the Bible. I knew absolutely nothing about Jesus or Christianity, so this was all new territory for me. As I sat quietly and listened to people talk about the unfailing love and forgiveness we can have in Christ, I was captivated. The idea that someone so kind, gentle, and loving would suffer and die so that *my* sins could be forgiven almost was too much to absorb. It gave me chills. There was something deeper going on inside me that I couldn't quite put my finger on at the time. Now I know: it was the first inkling of hope.

By the time the evening drew to a close, I was feeling better than I had in weeks. Although I didn't completely understand it, I was intrigued and encouraged by what I'd experienced that night. Not only did I enjoy being around these people, but I also was finding myself inexplicably drawn to the Bible. Sure, I still had a lot of questions, but there was one thing I was absolutely certain of—I would come back next week.

I became a regular at Wednesday night youth group after that. I even started attending Sunday morning services at Catalina's church, Central Christian. The more I attended, the more peace I felt. It was almost as if all the pain and sorrow I'd been harboring in my heart were being pushed aside by the warmth and love I now was experiencing. And this was only the beginning.

So when Central Christian announced that they were sponsoring a weeklong summer camp in Huntington Beach, California, I signed up to go. I had no idea what to expect, but I was fairly confident that whatever happened, it would be completely different from the two weeks I'd spent in Bangkok the previous summer.

And was it ever. In Thailand, everything revolved around external transformation. I spent almost all my time getting my hair done, getting my makeup done, doing countless wardrobe changes, posing to achieve a certain look—all things that disguised and concealed the real me. But my week in Huntington Beach was the exact opposite. Instead of the focus being on the physical side of me, it was all about spiritual transformation. For the first time in my life, I learned to look on the *inside* and discover my true identity in Christ. It would be years before I truly understood what that meant, but even so I was like a sponge, eagerly absorbing every word the speakers uttered.

Their message was simple, yet profound. All of us are born

sinners. In other words, we have a natural tendency to want to do things *our* way, as opposed to God's way. And our sin separates us from God. But because God loves us and doesn't want to be separated from us, He sent His Son, Jesus, to be a sacrifice on our behalf. Here's the amazing thing: Jesus' entire adult life was spent serving others—He fed the hungry, He clothed the poor, He healed the sick, and He comforted those who suffered. He also spoke the truth, openly challenging those who opposed God's ways. And for this, Jesus was brutally beaten, mocked, and killed.

But as Jesus was put to death on the cross, He responded with love and mercy. He took on the sins of all who come to Him for forgiveness. When Jesus rose from the dead three days later, it was proof that He had bridged the gap between God and people. Granted, we still are sinners. But if we believe in Jesus, commit ourselves to following His teaching and His example, and ask God's forgiveness for our sins, we will spend eternity with God as His children.

It all sounded so simple. Ask God for forgiveness, and you will be forgiven. And yet to me, it seemed impossible. I couldn't even forgive myself for what I had done. How could I possibly expect God to forgive me?

Ask God for forgiveness, and you will be forgiven. The phrase echoed in my head for hours—days, in fact. Finally, on the second-to-last day of camp, I couldn't ignore the tugging on my heart anymore. I had to confess to somebody, but I wasn't quite ready to talk to God yet. So I pulled aside our small group leader, Teresa. I had met Teresa at the first Wednesday night meeting I'd attended back in Las Vegas, and I felt more comfortable with her than anyone else at camp.

"I need to tell you something," I said. "I did something horrible." Suddenly I felt sick to my stomach.

"Whatever it is, God will forgive you," she assured me.

The tears started falling.

"But it's so bad, I can't even forgive myself," I choked out between sobs.

"It doesn't matter, Kylie. God still loves you, and He wants a relationship with you." She wrapped her arms around me and let me cry.

I swallowed hard, took a deep breath, and for the first time, told someone what had happened with Jake—about that horrible day and about every lie I'd both told and been told. Then I braced myself for the worst. I was so disgusted by what I'd done, and I couldn't imagine what Teresa thought of me.

But at that moment, I got my first taste of God's grace and forgiveness.

"None of that matters now." Teresa grabbed my hand and smiled warmly at me. "In spite of everything you're thinking and feeling right now, God does love you—more than you possibly can imagine. And He will forgive you. All you have to do is ask."

I so desperately wanted to believe her. I wanted to believe everything I'd heard that week. That God *did* love me and that He could forgive me for everything I'd done. But it still seemed impossible.

On the final night at camp, we all sat around a giant bonfire on the beach and sang worship songs. It was a beautiful evening—the perfect end to a life-changing week. As we were finishing the last song, our group leader walked around and handed each person a small piece of wood. He then challenged us to identify the one mistake or failure that we desperately wanted to have erased from our lives. He passed around some markers and told us to write that one thing on the wood. I grabbed one of the markers and stared blankly at my piece of wood. I knew what I wanted to write, but I couldn't bring myself to form the letters. Finally, my hands shaking, I scribbled, "Losing my virginity." It was so strange to see it there in writing.

"Okay," he announced, "now everyone take your piece of wood and throw it into the bonfire! On the count of three!"

Without even thinking, I stood and hurled that piece of wood as hard as I could into the flames.

I stared into the orange blaze, amazed at how liberated I felt. Even in that moment, I could tell that this would be a turning point for me. While the flames continued to lick the night air, literally consuming our deepest sins, fears, and insecurities, we bowed our heads as our leader said a closing prayer.

"God, You are the all-consuming fire," he began. "You are more holy and powerful than we can comprehend, and You are more loving and gracious than we can imagine. Thank You for taking all the parts of us that are broken and damaged, and for redeeming them into something beautiful."

I felt the heat of the fire flush my face. Of course the prayer was for everyone, but it felt like he was praying specifically about *me*.

"Thank You that when we bring our sins before You, You forgive us and make us whole again. Thank You that no sin we could commit, no mistake we ever could make, is a match for Your love—Your unconditional, unchanging love. As we leave this place, help us to grow deeper and stronger in You. Amen."

I still had a long way to go—and there would be plenty more pieces of wood I'd need to throw into the proverbial fire in the days and years ahead. But I had taken that first scary step. I had trusted God, by His grace, to forgive my sins, and I believed He would continue to guide me.

My spiritual journey had begun.

Chapter 7

NEW BEGINNINGS

Do not despise these small beginnings,
for the LORD rejoices to see the work begin.

ZECHARIAH 4:10, NLT

I RETURNED FROM Huntington Beach a different person. The cloud of misery and regret had been lifted, replaced by a new sense of joy and hope. I had officially put the episode with Jake behind me, and I was ready to move forward. In the past several months, I'd been granted the gift of new friends, a new perspective on life, and best of all, a new faith. I felt as though I'd been transformed from the inside out, and the change was almost palpable.

When I told Mom about everything I'd learned at camp—about the Bible and Christ's forgiveness and how God had changed my heart—her eyes glistened.

"I could tell there was something different about you the second I saw your face," she said. "You look so happy and"—she paused to find the right word—"peaceful. I feel like we've finally got the old Kylie back." She wrapped me in a warm hug.

It felt good to be close to Mom again. So good, in fact, that for a brief moment I was tempted to tell her about Jake. But I wasn't sure I was ready to reopen that wound yet.

"No, Mom," I whispered, burrowing my head into her hair like I used to when I was little. "You've got a brand-new Kylie back."

Over the next several weeks, I continued to share the things I'd learned at camp and the truths I was hearing at youth group with my mom, and before long God started opening her heart to Him too. Not only was I growing in my relationship with the Lord, but I was also getting closer to my mom. I couldn't remember ever being so happy.

In addition to attending church with me, Mom started following the teachings of Joyce Meyer, a popular Christian television personality and author. She liked to listen to Joyce's messages in the car, and from time to time I would listen to the CDs with her. Somewhat to my surprise, I liked Joyce. Her messages were always positive and upbeat, and they focused on personal restoration and turning your life around—which was exactly what I needed to hear at the time.

The rest of the summer passed in an endless blur of photo shoots, casting calls, and runway shows at the Fashion Show Mall. As much as I enjoyed the peaceful feeling that came over me at my weekly youth group meetings and Sunday services, I was still irrepressibly drawn to the bright lights and frenzied tempo of the modeling world.

Looking back, I guess you could say my life was a study in contrasts. I was equally attracted to two worlds that could not have been more diametrically opposed. The disconnect is crystal clear to me now, but back then, at the age of sixteen and with only a basic understanding of Christianity and the Bible, I couldn't see that those two paths would, at some point, put me on an inevitable collision course.

There was no question about it: I had changed a lot that summer. But I still had a long way to go. And I was about to discover that, despite the best intentions, some habits can be very difficult to break.

∽

"Guess what?" I called to my dad as he pulled into the driveway where I was practicing my dribbling skills.

"What?" He reached into the car, retrieving his briefcase from the backseat.

"I was working on my jump shot today after school, and I hit seven free throws in a row!" I couldn't hide my excitement.

"That's great, Kylie." Dad gave me a quick hug before breezing past me on his way inside. "Keep working on it," he called over his shoulder. "Practice makes perfect."

It wasn't exactly an all-star conversation. In fact, Dad barely even broke stride walking from the car to the house. Still, with things going so well with Mom now, I was hopeful that if I could make the basketball team that fall, maybe—just maybe—Dad would notice me and be proud of me again. It was the equivalent of a desperation shot at the buzzer, but since Dad hadn't shown any interest in coming to church with Mom and me, it was pretty much all I had left.

I worked my tail off getting ready for tryouts, and my efforts were rewarded when I made the junior varsity team. I also made a new friend in the process. His name was Lance. Like me, Lance was a sophomore who played basketball. And while he was good-looking like Jake, they had nothing else in common. Lance had no interest whatsoever in the party scene. He was honest, he wasn't a player, and most important, he was a Christian.

Lance and I hit it off immediately. Having learned from past experience, I was careful to keep our relationship at a friendship level as we were getting to know each other. We went to each other's games and cheered each other on. He even started coming to church with me. I was relieved to have our friendship out in the open—to know that my parents were not only aware of Lance; they adored him.

Another unexpected blessing came out of joining the basketball team: I was finally making a few good friends. I hadn't always had the best relationships with other girls at school, but between youth group and the basketball team, all of that seemed to be changing. As it happened, my best friend on the team was Lance's sister, Tatiana. She was a year younger than me, but she quickly became my closest confidant. The three of us went everywhere together—to the mall, to the movies, to church. I had never been this close to anyone besides my family before. And in a way, Lance and Tatiana felt like just that—family.

Things with Lance were everything my relationship with Jake hadn't been. Sweet. Innocent. Just right.

I couldn't imagine life getting any better than it was at that moment. I loved having friends who truly cared about me. I loved that my faith was growing, little by little. I loved playing basketball. And I loved that my parents were proud of me. My family came to every game, and it felt good to look in the stands and see them all sitting up there—especially my dad.

For the first time in ages, everything in my life seemed to be going perfectly. I barely had time to savor the moment, however. It was all about to evaporate with a single decision.

Chapter 8

RUDE AWAKENING

Turn to me and have mercy,
  for I am alone and in deep distress.
My problems go from bad to worse.
  Oh, save me from them all!
Feel my pain and see my trouble.
  Forgive all my sins.

PSALM 25:16-18, NLT

"I've got great news, Kylie!" Daniel, my agent at Envy, was positively beaming at me from across his desk. "We sent some of your print ad work to Vision Model Management in New York, and they loved it!"

When neither Mom nor I said anything, he continued. "They'd like to sign you. And this isn't just a one-time show or a weekend gig. They want you there full time."

I stared at him blankly, then glanced at my mom. Her expression mirrored mine—half excitement, half terror. It felt eerily similar to being in these very seats just over a year ago, when Daniel had told me about the opportunity to go to Thailand. This might be the big break I was hoping for . . . but at what cost?

Everything in my life had been going so well lately—at church, at school, in basketball, and with my family. How could I leave now?

But then again, how could I not? If I really wanted to give modeling a shot, I couldn't possibly let this chance pass me by.

"When would I need to be there?" I asked, finally finding my voice.

"As soon as possible," Daniel replied. Then he looked at my mom. "You're up for this . . . right?"

Mom exhaled deeply. "We'll have to discuss it as a family."

Even though New York City was much closer than Thailand, this felt bigger, scarier. The Thailand gig was only temporary. And Mom could go with me. This, however, was long term. And I would be going all by myself. My head was spinning.

"Thank you, Daniel," Mom said, standing and collecting her things. "We'll let you know our decision as soon as possible."

"I understand." He rose to shake Mom's hand. "But they'll need an answer quickly."

Then he looked straight at me. "This is the chance of a lifetime."

I don't think anyone in our house got a wink of sleep that night. All through dinner and late into the evening, Mom, Dad, and I discussed the ramifications of my moving to New York. I was honest about my reservations—I didn't want to leave my friends at church and at school, I hated the idea of quitting the basketball team, and I was afraid to be all on my own in New York without friends or family nearby.

But at the same time, I made a case for why I should go. By industry standards, I was already pushing the envelope age-wise.

Most serious models were doing New York fashion shows by the age of fifteen or sixteen, and if you hadn't broken out by the time you were eighteen, odds were that your career pretty much was over. I knew this was really a case of now or never.

As for school, I had always been a good student, so I didn't see any reason why I couldn't finish my classes online. My parents knew I was serious about modeling as a career, so it wasn't as though this was just some short-lived teenage whim.

We discussed the pros and cons for hours, and long after I'd gone to bed, I could still hear my parents talking through the wall of my bedroom.

When I emerged for breakfast the following morning, though, everyone was quiet.

It was my mom who broke the silence. "Kylie, your father and I have decided to let you go to New York. But . . ." Before she could even finish her sentence, I flew across the room and wrapped both of them in a huge hug.

"Thank you!" I squealed, fighting the urge to jump up and down. They were, after all, treating me like an adult, so it was in my best interest to try to act like one.

Mom continued, "But we're going to hold you to your commitment of finishing your course work online."

"I will. I definitely will," I promised. "Can I call Daniel now and tell him to let VMM know I said yes?"

Mom and Dad exchanged a glance, as if they were giving each other one last chance to change their minds. Then they nodded.

"Thank you!" I raced back to my room to make the biggest phone call of my career.

Now that the decision had been made, my fears had all but vanished. I was elated. But I also knew how difficult this was for my parents. It would have been one thing for me to move out to go to college, but I wasn't even seventeen. And I wasn't going to a campus full of dorms and academic buildings; I was moving all the way across the country, diving headfirst into the unknown world of professional modeling. Still, in spite of their hesitations, and as much as they wished I could get my big break right there in Vegas, they knew that New York was the next stepping-stone for me to achieve my heart's desire—and neither of them wanted to deny me that chance. I was their little girl, and they wanted me to have the world.

Of course, at sixteen and a half, I had no idea how harsh the world could be.

The next few days were a frenzied blur of packing and good-byes. Lance and I officially broke up but vowed to keep in touch. I hugged my friends from youth group and the girls on my basketball team, Tatiana included. We promised to talk whenever we could.

Before I left, my dad gave me a cylinder of pepper spray and made me promise to carry it at all times. I told him I would, reminding him that he'd done a good job of teaching me how to defend myself. I was confident I could wrestle an attacker to the ground and even get off a good blow to the jugular, if need be.

To help set my parents' minds at ease, Daniel accompanied me to New York to introduce me to my new employer and make sure I got off on the right foot. I was glad he did. As we walked into the VMM office in Manhattan, I tried to give off a confident air, but in truth, I'd never been so intimidated and nervous in all my life.

Once inside, I smiled politely, nodding through the pleasant-ries. Then I was informed I'd be sharing an apartment on the Lower West Side with four other models.

"Four?" I blurted without thinking.

"Yes." My new boss, Stephen, was distractedly leafing through a pile of papers. He handed a card with the apartment's address to Daniel. "The other girls are all represented by VMM. Don't worry. I'm sure you'll fit right in."

I hoped he was right. But from what I'd seen of the city so far, I had a hard time imagining myself fitting in with *anyone* in Manhattan.

After we left VMM, Daniel gave me a quick tutorial on the subway system, showed me how to find Penn Station and Grand Central Station, and gave me an overview of the different bor-oughs and neighborhoods where I'd likely be working. Then we set off for my new apartment on foot.

New York City was even more impressive than I'd imagined it would be, and it made Vegas seem like Jackpot by compari-son. I'd seen dozens of movies and TV shows that took place in Manhattan, but seeing it on-screen couldn't compare to standing right in the middle of it. New York wasn't just huge; it also was loud and fast. And the buzz was infectious. I could practically feel the rhythm of the city pulsating in my veins.

"Thank You, God," I whispered. "Thank You for giving me this opportunity."

There was one thing about New York I wasn't prepared for, however. As we made our way across the Lower West Side, I was struck by the number of homeless people we passed. They seemed to be everywhere—leaning up against the sides of buildings, sit-ting in doorways, even sleeping on the sidewalks.

Don't people notice them? I wondered as I watched everyone hurry past without so much as a passing glance. I wished I could do something, but with barely enough money to afford even the most basic essentials and no idea when my first paying job would come, I wasn't in much of a position to help anyone.

I was so lost in my own thoughts that I barely noticed when Daniel stopped in front of an old apartment building just off East Third Street and Avenue C. It didn't look very clean, and there was a distinct aroma of garbage in the air.

"Is this it?" I asked, half hoping the answer would be no.

"Let's find out." Daniel opened the outer door and stopped in front of the apartment that read 57C.

"Yep. This is it." He turned the key and opened the door.

I followed him inside, lingering behind a bit.

"Hello," he called out. "Anybody home?"

The lights were on, but there was no answer. I took a quick look around, trying to hide my disappointment. The place was small—very small—but I'd heard that most apartments in NYC were pretty tiny, so I tried not to be too critical. From what I could see, there were two small bedrooms—one with a single twin bed and the other with two sets of bunk beds. One of the bunk bed spots was empty, presumably reserved for me. There was one tiny bathroom and a small kitchen that opened into a little living room–type space. Not much elbow room for four girls plus the twenty-four-year-old woman who had been assigned by the agency to be our chaperone.

This is going to be interesting, I thought.

"Well, Kylie." Daniel turned to me with a sense of finality. "I hate to say it, but I really need to get going if I'm going to catch my flight." As if sensing my apprehension, he came over and gave me a quick hug. "You'll be fine," he whispered. "Now make us proud," he added with a wink at me. And then he was gone.

I set my suitcases on the empty bunk bed and started to unpack. The first items I pulled out were the pictures of my parents and Luke I'd taken right before I left. As soon as I saw their faces smiling at me, my throat constricted, and I could feel tears burning at the corners of my eyes. It had been less than twelve hours since I'd said good-bye to them at the airport, but it seemed like a lifetime. I set down the frames on the nightstand next to the bed and positioned them so my family's faces would be the last thing I saw before I fell asleep at night and the first thing to greet me when I woke up in the morning. Then I unpacked my Bible and the Joyce Meyer CDs my mom had given me.

God, please help me to do well here, I prayed silently. *Let me make my family and all the people back in Vegas proud of me.*

Suddenly a cheerful voice pierced the silence. "We pretty much just live out of our suitcases here." I looked up to see a tall, pretty girl about my age walking into the room.

"Hi." She smiled at me and stretched out her hand. "I'm Breanna."

"I'm Kylie." I stood to greet her, still holding my Bible.

"Are you a Christian?" she asked, eyeing my Bible.

"Yeah," I responded sheepishly, not sure how something like that would go over in New York.

"Really?" Breanna asked, smiling even wider. "Me, too."

Thank You, God. I exhaled deeply.

Breanna and I talked a little more as I continued to unpack. It turned out we had a lot in common. We both came from small towns. We'd both played basketball in high school, and we both had a weakness for ice cream.

As I climbed under the covers that night, I was exhausted yet hopeful. What had started out as a tear-filled day of good-byes had ended with the promise of new adventures on the horizon—a new opportunity, a new city, and a new friend.

Just before drifting off, I took one last glance at the smiling faces of my mom, my dad, and my little brother. Then I closed my eyes and prayed. *Thank You, God, for keeping me safe today and for giving me a Christian roommate. Please be with me tomorrow as I take the next step toward achieving my dream. And please look after all those who aren't fortunate enough to have a warm bed to sleep in tonight.*

The agency apartment might not have been much, but as I had already discovered on my first day in New York, it was more than a lot of people had.

The following day was filled with test shoot after test shoot. I needed to build my photo portfolio, so the agency booked me for several photo shoots, all in different locations. And so, armed with only a subway map, my trusty pepper spray, and a sense of adventure, I embarked upon my New York modeling career.

For the first round of test shoots, the agency booked local photographers, and the photos turned out great. At least *I* thought so. Stephen, my new handler, gently pointed out that several of the shots showed off my muscular build a little too much, and he reminded me that the most successful high-fashion models didn't look athletic. Their customers wanted a more willowy look. Translation: I was too heavy.

Stephen wasted no time in telling me I needed to cut out the weight training and just focus on cardio workouts. In other words,

I had to lose some of the "bulk" I'd acquired from my high school basketball days and my weight-training classes. Since I barely had enough time or money to eat and I was walking sixty to eighty blocks a day going from test shoot to test shoot, I figured I had both bases covered. If making it as a model hinged on being rail thin, I was determined to do whatever it took to get that look.

Meanwhile, Breanna and I continued to bond. From my very first day, she took me under her wing and helped me in every way she could. She made sure I knew where I was going, helped me select the best photos for my portfolio, and told me which subway stops to avoid after dark. She even took me to church with her on Sundays. I truly believe God put Breanna in my life during what would prove to be a challenging season. She was a godly example and a role model for me—which was more than I could say for our other two roommates.

Breanna and I didn't see the other two girls who lived with us very often. One of the girls pretty much kept to herself. Our other roommate left almost every night in a black SUV and didn't return to the apartment until 2 or 3 a.m., even though we all had test shoots or casting calls the next morning. She was only seventeen, so I didn't know what she was doing every night into the wee hours of the morning. Then one day as I was heading out for a jog, I saw the trademark black SUV parked out front. My roommate was already climbing inside, when a guy I'd never seen before called out the window, "Hey, do you want to come with us?"

"Where are you going?" I asked, dying to know where she'd been each night.

"Clubbing," he called back.

I wasn't even sure I knew what that meant.

"We'll wait if you want to change your clothes."

"Thanks, but I don't think so." I grabbed my left heel to stretch my hamstring.

"Come on," he pressed. "You can eat for free at one of New York's finest restaurants, plus all the alcohol you want. All you have to do is mingle and look beautiful. What do you say?"

At that point, my roommate glared at me from inside the vehicle, as if to say, "Don't even think about it." But she had nothing to worry about. I didn't want any part of that deal.

"No thanks." I turned away and headed off on my jog. The party scene didn't appeal to me—I just wanted to model.

How in the world is she eating and drinking like that and staying so thin? I wondered as I watched the SUV speed off into the night. *I'm barely eating anything and I work out around the clock, and I'm still getting labeled as "bulky."*

Despite the fact that I was a bit curvier than some of the other models in the agency, I was still booking a number of jobs. That's why I was surprised when Stephen sent me on yet another test shoot my third week in NYC. My portfolio was already packed, and it showcased a wide variety of looks, from casual and out-doorsy to high-end formal. *What could I possibly be missing?* I wondered.

When I arrived at the photographer's apartment, there were still a few other models ahead of me, so I went into the other room to have my hair and makeup done.

As the stylist was finishing up, the photographer called from the other room, "Is she ready?"

The stylist took a step back and looked at me. She looked bored. Or unhappy. Or both.

"Yep," she called back, giving my hair a final shot of hair spray.

When I got into the next room, I was a little surprised to find that the photographer was significantly older than the ones I'd worked with in the past. Most test shoot photographers are young guns just starting out. They're trying to build their portfolios just like new models are, so it's not so much about the money as it is about getting experience. And like models, if a photographer hasn't broken in by his late twenties, odds are he's never going to. This guy appeared to be in his midforties.

His age wasn't the only thing that was odd about him, though. His hair was long, kind of greasy, and pulled back into a ponytail, and when I came in the room, he looked me up and down in a way that made me feel . . . uncomfortable. I couldn't put my finger on what it was, but something just seemed off about him.

"Just hit some standard poses," he instructed, taking his position a few feet away.

At least this will be a quick and easy shoot, I thought. It was pretty standard—I just had on a white tank top and jeans, so the focus would be on my face and my body as opposed to the clothing or accessories.

I ran my fingers through my hair and tilted my head back, looking seductively at the camera lens, the way I'd been taught in Vegas.

The photographer took a few more shots and then stopped. "Wait right here. I want to try something." When he left the room, I shook out my arms a little and leaned forward in a deep squat to loosen up my muscles and relax a little. I could hear someone opening cabinets in the kitchen area, and I figured the stylist was making a fresh pot of coffee. Seconds later, though, the photographer came back holding a box of Saran Wrap. I immediately shot up into a standing position. I felt my stomach start to churn.

This can't be good.

"Take off your shirt and wrap this around your top," he said matter-of-factly, handing me the Saran Wrap.

I stood perfectly still. *I'm sure I didn't hear that right.*

"Go ahead," he said. "Take off your bra, too. This will be perfect for your book—very artistic."

He had to be kidding. No other model I knew had pictures like this in her portfolio. I just stood there, my eyes wide with shock.

He was starting to get frustrated with me. "Do you want me to call your agency and tell them you can't handle it?"

That snapped me back to reality. My cheeks flushed, and my mind started racing. *Stephen already thinks I'm too bulky to make it in New York. And clearly he thought something was missing from my portfolio, or he wouldn't have sent me out again.*

Then the paranoia kicked in. VMM had booked this shoot—was this some kind of a test to see if I had what it took to be a high-end fashion model? What if I said no and this guy called the agency? Would they drop me? I knew nobody wanted to represent a model with a reputation for being difficult to work with.

My fears exploded into full-blown panic. *I can't go home a failure after only three weeks. Mom and Dad and everyone at Envy are counting on me. I can't disappoint them. I can't!*

And so, with almost robotic movements, I took the Saran Wrap box from the photographer's outstretched hand and disappeared into the bathroom. I didn't look at myself in the mirror. I couldn't. With my throat burning and my eyes stinging with tears, I slipped off my top and my bra and began wrapping my chest in the see-through material. I felt nauseous. It was the same feeling I'd had in Jake's car that afternoon right before everything fell apart. I definitely was not comfortable with this, and yet at that moment, the intense compulsion not to be rejected or to be labeled difficult or uncooperative somehow outweighed my values and my common sense. That's how the enemy works—through manipulation, fear, and self-doubt. And that afternoon, I was firmly in his grasp.

Just then the bathroom door opened and the photographer was standing there. "What's taking so long?" he demanded. Then he looked at me with an air of exasperation. "No—you're doing it wrong. Here, let me help." He grabbed the Saran Wrap and started tucking and pulling at it.

It was a nightmare. I wanted to melt right into the floor. He kept touching my chest, trying to get the Saran Wrap into just the right position "so it would photograph nicely." I couldn't even get any words out. I just wanted him to stop.

After what felt like an eternity, he said gruffly, "Okay, let's try some shots." His camera clicked away as I tried to hit different poses while simultaneously covering my chest with my arms.

"No!" he snapped. "That's not the look I want."

Please, make it stop!

"Follow me," he said, leading me back toward the bathroom. "I'll show you what I want."

Trying desperately to remain professional, I followed him.

"It'll be easier if you practice the look I want in front of the mirror."

I still couldn't bear to face myself, but he wasn't giving me a choice.

Reaching from behind me, he lifted my face until I was staring straight ahead.

My eyes met his eyes in the mirror. He was looking at me like no other photographer had looked at me before. Panic set in. I prepared to make a break for it, but then he trapped me against the bathroom wall and tried to kiss me. I shoved him away, but my arms were shaking violently and my legs felt like rubber. He quickly moved in again.

"Shh. Shh. It's okay. It's okay," he hushed, pressing up against me.

"No, it's *not* okay," I spat back, pushing him away with all my might.

I didn't knock him down, but I did manage to put enough distance between us to duck under his arm and bolt out of the bathroom. I quickly grabbed my top and pulled it on over the Saran Wrap, snatched my purse, and rushed out of the apartment. I breezed past the stylist, who was jamming to Avril Lavigne, totally oblivious to what was going on.

I took off down the stairs and out the door, and I kept running for almost two blocks before stopping to catch my breath. Strangely, nobody seemed to think the sight of a young girl sprinting down the street covered in plastic wrap and crying was worth noticing. Such was life in the big city, I was learning. There were millions of people around, yet in many ways, I was completely alone.

As soon as I got back to the apartment, I immediately took a shower, and then, still shaking, I called my mom. I could barely speak through the sobs, but eventually I was able to relay the whole sordid story.

Mom was appalled. "I'm so sorry, baby. Are you sure you're okay? Are you sure he didn't hurt you?" She sounded panicked.

I assured her I was fine—just frightened and embarrassed. She asked if I wanted to come home, and for an instant, I considered it. I missed Mom terribly, and with the exception of Breanna and a smattering of small print jobs, New York was not turning out to be the glamorous thrill ride I had imagined it to be. And yet, in spite of what had just happened, I wasn't ready to give up.

"No, Mom," I answered. "I'm fine, really. It was just a terrible day." I paused for a second, wondering if I'd convinced her. To be honest, though, I wasn't entirely sure I'd convinced myself.

Mom sighed deeply, then said, "Okay. If you're absolutely sure. But I'm calling your agent first thing in the morning, and we're going to get to the bottom of this. Dream job or not, I will not have anyone putting your safety at risk." Mom was still angry, but I could hear the resignation in her voice. I would be staying in New York.

When Breanna got home, I told her what had happened. Being the good friend she was, she was almost as upset as my mom had been. Then she did what my mom wanted so desperately to do but couldn't—she gave me a big hug. She didn't let go until I had cried myself to sleep.

The next day, as promised, Mom called VMM and unleashed her wrath on Stephen, who apologized profusely and promised to deal with the photographer personally. But first he called me.

"Kylie, are you okay?" Stephen asked, clearly still shaken by my mom's tongue-lashing.

"I'm fine," I assured him. "It was really awful, though. That guy shouldn't even be allowed near models."

"I am so, so sorry, Kylie. We had no idea," he said. "If you ever feel uncomfortable or pressured by a photographer like that again, I want you to call me immediately. I'll handle it."

And handle it he did. The agency removed the photographer from their list and promised to never work with him again. Ironically, by threatening to ruin my reputation, he had ruined his own.

As for me, I'd gotten my first glimpse of the seedy underside of the modeling industry. I had been presented with my first real test on my way to the top, and I had failed. Miserably. Once again, I'd let my fear of rejection force me into a situation I knew was wrong. I had compromised my values for the sake of being liked and accepted. And I'd suffered horrific consequences as a result.

The only real silver lining was that I'd learned I had a genuine friend in Breanna. I was also encouraged by how quickly Stephen and the others at VMM had come to my defense. But I was quickly discovering that the modeling industry wasn't at all what I thought it would be. My eyes were being opened to some harsh realities. And they were about to be opened even wider.

Chapter 9

EYES WIDE OPEN

We fix our eyes not on what is seen,
but on what is unseen, since what is seen
is temporary, but what is unseen is eternal.

2 CORINTHIANS 4:18

DETERMINED NOT TO LET the behavior of one sleazy photographer crush my spirit, I threw myself into my work, attending one casting call after another in preparation for the industry's biggest event of the year—New York Fashion Week.

Every February, the top designers in the world descend on New York City to show off their newest lines, attracting swarms of celebrities and paparazzi and catapulting a select handful of fresh faces to instant supermodel status. It was the fashion industry's equivalent of the Academy Awards, and like hundreds of other young hopefuls, I was eager to be invited to the party. For two weeks I tramped through the icy, frostbitten streets of greater Manhattan, auditioning for every designer from American Eagle to Vera Wang. It was exhausting and exhilarating all at once.

These auditions were the first real chance I'd gotten since arriving in New York to see my competition up close, and I felt my confidence plummeting by the minute. Having dropped almost six pounds since Stephen's mandate that I lose "the bulk," I went into Fashion Week auditions weighing in at a meager 115 pounds. At five feet ten, that was the thinnest I'd ever been, yet compared to some of the models I was running into at the castings, I looked huge. And they made sure I knew it. I expected the competition to be fierce, but I'd never encountered this level of cattiness. I tried to thicken my skin, but the comments from some of the other models bordered on abusive.

The designers weren't shy about sharing their opinions either. I was experiencing new levels of humiliation—going out on a runway and giving my best effort, only to be greeted by a chorus of exasperated sighs from the darkened auditorium and by snickers of laughter from the other models backstage. It seemed that for every designer who was complimentary of my look and my walk, five or six others felt I was "too curvy" or "too big." And when these criticisms were received en masse over the course of a five-day period, the overall experience was pretty demoralizing.

Even more disheartening were the pictures I saw on a lot of the other models' comp cards—two-sided 6x9 glossy sheets that featured two or three of their best looks from their portfolios on one side and their height, weight, measurements, and contact info on the other. Almost all the cards included at least one topless pose, and in some cases, the models were completely nude. I was stunned. I thought the Saran Wrap incident was an isolated case of one sick individual taking advantage of a young girl who was new to the business. But I was starting to wonder if, at this level, topless or nude poses were actually standard practice.

What does posing nude have to do with fashion? I wondered. And yet the models with the R-rated comp cards seemed to be the ones getting the jobs.

After all I'd seen at auditions, I barely held out hope that one of the companies might be interested in me. So I was shocked when Stephen called from VMM to tell me I'd been cast in not just one but *seven* different runway shows.

I was ecstatic. After a miserable couple of weeks, I felt like I was turning a corner. Maybe I was finally on my way to making something of myself in this industry.

As soon as I hung up with Stephen, I called my mom to tell her the news.

"Mom, guess what?"

"What?" She sounded hesitant. I guess she had reason to be on her guard, especially after the last call she'd gotten from me.

"I'm walking in Fashion Week next month! I'll be in seven different shows!" I couldn't hold in my excitement. "Can you believe it?"

"Oh, honey, that's fantastic!" I could practically hear Mom beaming over the phone. "I am so proud of you."

"Will you or Dad be able to come?" I asked. I knew that at least one of them would have to stay home with Luke.

"Well, your dad is very busy with work right now." Her words sounded like an apology. "But I'd love to be there. Just send me the dates, and I'll book my flight right away."

I couldn't have been happier at the prospect of seeing her. In fact, I was almost more excited about that than about Fashion Week itself.

That night, after texting Mom the dates, I climbed into bed, exhausted but happy. I hadn't felt this elated since the night in Huntington Beach when God had opened my heart to His truth.

As I thought about that night at youth group camp, I felt a pang of regret. It had been a while since I'd read my Bible or gone to church. Or even talked to God, for that matter. It was so much harder to focus on my faith and my relationship with God now that I was alone in New York. Back in Vegas, I'd had my church and my youth group to help me study and understand the Bible, and I had friends like Lance and Tatiana to keep me on track. Breanna had taken me to church with her a few times, but those Sundays were few and far between. Every once in a while, when I couldn't sleep, I would put on my headphones and listen to one of the Joyce Meyer CDs my mom had given me. But it wasn't the same as digging into the Word myself.

My faith was only a few months old, and there still was so much I didn't know. Becoming a Christian and then immediately taking off for the New York modeling scene was like learning how to hold your breath underwater one day and then trying to swim the English Channel the next. I knew the basics, but I was hardly prepared to venture into the deep end.

There was no way around it: God had taken a backseat to my career.

Fashion Week was shaping up to be everything I'd expected— and then some. Celebrities from all around the world had flown in for this seven-day extravaganza filled with fashion shows, red-carpet events, and A-list parties. The fact that both my mom and Breanna's mom had flown in for the event made the experience even more meaningful.

As soon as Mom saw me, she gasped at how much weight I'd lost.

"Kylie, you look so gaunt." She couldn't keep the concern from creeping into her voice. "Are you eating enough?"

"I'm fine, Mom," I assured her. "I just cut out the carbs and kicked up my cardio workouts a little. I'll be able to slow it down after Fashion Week is over." I wasn't sure how true that statement was, but it set Mom's mind at ease for the moment. I wanted her to enjoy this week, not spend the whole time worrying about me.

Thank goodness Mom didn't see what happened backstage at the shows, or she would have been *really* worried.

While everything looked perfectly choreographed out on the runway, it was chaos behind the scenes. In every square inch there were half-naked models—both male and female—pushing, shoving, and frantically grabbing at dressing racks. Women staggered around in stilettos that were two inches too high and two sizes too small while hostile designers threw tantrums over gowns that weren't draping quite right and pants that were bunching up in all the wrong places.

Hairstylists tore out extensions, filled the air with toxic clouds of hair spray, and scorched models' scalps alternately with piping hot curling irons and flat irons. Makeup artists ripped off false eyelashes, yanked out eyebrows, and nearly blinded models with airbrushes. Everywhere you looked, it was absolute bedlam. There wasn't an inch of privacy, and there was virtually no compassion or respect shown for the models who were sacrificing their bodies for the sake of a sixty-second walk down the runway.

To my relief, the styling for my American Eagle show went relatively smoothly. Their clothes tend to be more casual and sporty, which was similar to how I dressed anyway, so the backstage work didn't require as much of a total transformation as some of the other labels.

I'll never forget the feeling of anticipation as I waited for my cue to take the stage. My heart felt as if it were going to burst right out of my chest. This wasn't just some weekend back-to-school show at the mall in Vegas; this was Fashion Week in New York.

This was the big time.

When the stagehand pointed at me and said, "Go!" I took a deep breath, rounded the corner, and walked onto the runway. The music was deafening, and the nonstop camera flashes were so blinding I could barely see where I was going. Yet I was in my element. In an instant, all my feelings of doubt and insecurity evaporated. They were replaced with the absolute certainty that this was where I belonged—out on the runway, doing my thing, with all eyes on me. As I walked down that runway, there was no question in my mind. I was born to be a model.

And truth be told, I loved the actual modeling portion of the shows. It was everything else that came with it that I hated. For example, in one of the shows I did that week, the designer decided he wanted me to have an extreme, Lady Gaga–type look, so the stylist tied my hair into a giant bow and absolutely slathered it with a mixture of styling gel, paste, and putty to hold it in place. I have to admit they pulled off the look, but for every second I spent on stage, it felt like I spent about an hour trying to wash that crazy concoction out of my hair. Another night, the stylist held a flat iron on my hair so long it actually started smoking. By the time she finished, my hair was literally fried to a crisp. It didn't matter to the stylist, though. She knew that if she didn't like the way it looked, she could always throw in some extensions to cover up the mess. She wouldn't have to deal with the damage, which lasted for months.

In one of my final shows of the week, the designer wanted an ultra-dramatic look, so the stylist started gluing false eyelashes onto my lids. It wasn't until my eyes started burning and tears started streaming down my face that I realized she was using permanent glue.

"It burns like battery acid," she said matter-of-factly. "But it's the best glue in the world when it comes to making sure those lashes stay put."

By the time she was finished, I had to admit the lashes looked gorgeous. And it was a good thing I liked them because no matter how hard I scrubbed, I couldn't get them off. I tried everything—soap, cold cream, makeup remover—but every product I tried was powerless against the miracle glue. Eventually my eyes became so red and irritated that I resorted to pulling out the lashes by hand. Unfortunately, when they finally came out, they took my real lashes with them. I looked horrible. It was more than a month before my natural eyelashes started to grow back in again. Even now, several years later, they're nowhere near as thick or as long as they used to be. I used to wonder about the origin of the expression "Beauty is pain." Now I have no doubt the phrase was first uttered backstage during a fashion show.

Aside from my charred and gooey hair and the unremovable eyelashes, my first Fashion Week went off without a hitch. I wasn't plucked from obscurity to become the next Heidi Klum or Tyra Banks, but I had proven my mettle among some of the best models in the industry and, for the most part, had enjoyed the experience.

The icing on the cake was the time I'd been able to spend with my mom. It had been so good to see her, which made it all the more difficult to say good-bye.

"You looked so beautiful up there," Mom gushed, her eyes glistening. "I don't know when I've been more proud of you."

"Thanks, Mom." I wrapped my arms around her in a tight hug and felt my own eyes starting to tear up.

"I wish your father could have been here to see you."

I let out a sigh. "Me, too." I wanted Dad to be proud of me. *There will be other shows,* I told myself. I was too busy to dwell on it long, and besides, the glow of the spotlight hadn't faded yet.

I was still riding the high of Fashion Week when Breanna came back to the apartment one afternoon with terrible news.

"It's bad, Kylie. Really bad." She was so choked up she could barely get the words out. Finally she told me the whole dreadful story.

It turned out that the owners of Vision Model Management had decided to close up shop, and they took off overnight with all the company's cash, leaving the models, bookers, agents, and handlers with nothing.

"What about the money we earned during Fashion Week?" I sputtered. "Aren't we entitled to that?"

She shook her head. "That's not the worst of it. We have to be out of the apartment immediately."

I felt like I'd been robbed in broad daylight. I'd forgotten that the agency owned the apartment and deducted the rent from whatever money we made—however much that was. In the two months I'd been in New York, I hadn't seen a single dime from any of the jobs I'd done. Everything went through the agency. In addition to the rent, they deducted agency fees, the cost of our portfolios, and whatever other expenses they deemed necessary. We were completely at their mercy.

Less than twenty-four hours ago I was walking the runway at Fashion Week. Now I had no job, no money, and no place to live.

Breanna and I both called our moms and broke the bad news. Like us, they were angry yet powerless. Seeing no other choice, Breanna and I packed up our things while our moms made arrangements for us to return home.

"Well, it was fun while it lasted." Breanna stood in front of me solemnly, suitcase in hand.

"I'll miss you." I tried in vain not to cry. "You've been a great friend."

"We'll keep in touch," she promised. "After all, Nebraska isn't that far from Vegas."

We gave each other a final hug and went our separate ways. I never did see Breanna again. I don't know if she made her way back to New York or if she even stayed in the industry, for that matter.

Either way, my illusions about the glamorous world of modeling were crumbling before my eyes. Now that I was seeing what happened behind the scenes, I realized what a lonely and unscrupulous business modeling can be. In just a matter of months, I'd been lied to, taken advantage of, insulted, and almost assaulted. Now I was on my way back home with nothing to show for my trouble except a few credentials on my résumé and some new shots for my portfolio.

But there was one more thing I was leaving with. In spite of all the negative things that had happened, I was leaving New York with a renewed conviction that I was born to be a model. I had seen how harsh and distasteful the industry could be at the bottom. *Surely,* I thought, *things must be better at the top.*

Chapter 10

REBOUNDING

Your heart was filled with pride
because of all your beauty.
Your wisdom was corrupted
by your love of splendor.

EZEKIEL 28:17, NLT

WHEN I PLAYED BASKETBALL, my coaches taught me that whenever I missed a shot, I should put myself in position to make the most of whatever happened next. So as soon as I got home, Mom and I went to see Daniel at Envy to find out what would give me the best chance of getting back to New York. To our surprise, the most direct route from Las Vegas to New York was through Osaka.

"I can get you a gig in Japan," Daniel informed me, "provided you can leave right away."

"Japan?" I didn't even try to hide my shock. "How long would I have to stay?"

"About two months." He shot Mom an apologetic glance. "It's worth it, though. You can make some great money there, which will help offset what you lost with VMM. And when you get back, we can see about placing you with another agency in New York. What do you think?"

My mind immediately flashed back to the hot, crowded streets of Bangkok and the unsavory scene at the Pizza Hut. I could tell by the expression on Mom's face that she was thinking the exact same thing.

Sensing our hesitancy, Daniel quickly added, "It's really the best option if you want to keep your career moving in the right direction."

I looked at Mom again, noticing that she suddenly appeared exhausted.

"We'll talk about it tonight and get back to you tomorrow," she replied, reaching for her purse. "Thank you, Daniel."

"You're welcome." Daniel rose to shake her hand. "And, Kylie, I'm really sorry about what happened in New York."

"Thanks, Daniel," I said, offering him a small smile. I knew it wasn't his fault that VMM had folded, but between the Bangkok disappointment and the nightmare in New York, I was starting to get a little leery of all the so-called great opportunities people kept promising me.

Mom and I had been in the car for almost ten minutes before I finally broke the silence.

"I think I should go." I looked out the passenger window. "I'm older now. I'll be okay."

"You haven't even been home twenty-four hours, Kylie. You've been through a lot these past few weeks, and with everything that has happened, I just don't feel right about sending you off again." Mom stared straight ahead. "New York is one thing, but Japan? You don't speak the language, you don't know anything about the culture, and there's no way I could leave Luke for that long. You'd be completely on your own."

"But this might be the only way I can get back to New York," I countered.

No response.

"I'm caught up with all my credits at school," I continued. "And going back to the Fashion Mall would be like taking a giant step backward at this point. It would be like all the hard work I did in New York was for nothing."

She didn't say anything, but I sensed that she was weakening. Finally, after what seemed like an eternal silence, she said, "Okay. But I don't want you going by yourself. Let me give your grandma a call and see if she can go with you."

I breathed a sigh of relief. "Thank you, Mom. And don't worry. Everything will be fine. I promise." I leaned my head against the headrest, smiling. I was still anxious about going to Japan, but at least my career was back on track.

Just a two-month stopover in Japan and I'll be back in New York by June, I thought. *And this time, everything's going to be different.*

I had barely unpacked my bags before I was back on a plane headed for Osaka, a bustling city of 2.5 million people and my home for the next two months. Since my grandma didn't have time to get a passport before I left, I had to go solo for the first two weeks while she waited on the necessary paperwork. It was a little unnerving to be starting out in a foreign city on my own, but I put on a brave face for my parents' sake. They were already nervous enough as it was.

The long flight gave me plenty of time to worry. After several failed attempts at sleep, I grabbed my headphones so I could listen to one of my favorite Joyce Meyer CDs. As Joyce preached about the power to overcome anxiety and fear, I slowly began to relax. *I can do this,* I assured myself over and over again. *I can do this.* I was missing one of the key points about what it meant to be a Christian—that it wasn't about overcoming anxiety for my own sake but about living fearlessly so I could serve Christ. It wasn't just about positive feelings because, as was evident from the lives of Jesus' disciples, we aren't guaranteed an easy life. I was right that God wanted me to overcome my fears, but my motivations were all wrong.

I had just about convinced myself that everything was going to be fine and that I was going to take Osaka by storm when the pilot came over the intercom and announced that we were beginning our descent. I felt a flutter of nerves deep in my stomach. *Please, God, help me make it through the next two months.*

Upon landing at the airport, I picked up my luggage and dug through my purse for the slip of paper Daniel had given me. The instructions were simple, yet intimidating.

1. Buy a token.
2. Go to the ground transportation area and find the bus.
3. Get off the bus, find a taxi, and hand the driver this slip of paper. The apartment address is on the back.
4. Good luck!

I managed to find the token machine and navigate the bus system easily enough. After I got off the bus, it took me only a few minutes to hail a cab. Unfortunately, that's where my luck ran out. Communicating with the cabdriver was a nightmare. He spoke about as much English as I spoke Japanese, but I could tell by his body language that he didn't have the slightest idea how to get to the address Daniel had provided. The driver kept asking me questions in Japanese, and I just kept pointing to the address on the piece of paper. It was late. I was tired. And we were getting nowhere fast. Finally, he waved his hand, muttered something unintelligible into his two-way radio, and pulled away from the curb. I had no idea where we were going, and I had a strong suspicion he didn't either.

After what seemed like an hour, the driver pulled up in front of an apartment complex and pointed.

"Is this it?" I asked.

He pointed at the slip of paper and nodded, then pointed at the meter. I was flabbergasted. The total came to more than $100!

I had a strong hunch I'd just been taken for a ride—both literally and figuratively—but by that point I was too exhausted to argue. I'd been traveling for almost two days, and I just wanted to get inside, take a shower, and collapse into bed.

After handing over almost half the money in my wallet, I grabbed my bags out of the trunk and dragged everything toward the complex. Key in hand, I strained my exhausted eyes, trying to find my apartment number. *Could this day get any harder?*

"There it is," I announced triumphantly after finally arriving at the right door.

Daniel had said that I'd have my own studio apartment, which was a welcome relief after the cramped living quarters back in New York. Once inside, I flipped on the lights, only to discover that I *did* have roommates after all—dozens of them! Cockroaches the size of sugar packets scattered across the floor, scurrying under the bed, the refrigerator, and the stove. Had I actually eaten anything in the past eighteen hours, I probably would have lost all of it in that moment.

Eventually my exhaustion overrode my disgust, and with my unexpected houseguests momentarily out of sight, I unpacked my suitcases, took a quick shower, and climbed into bed. Since the roaches seemed to prefer the darkness, I pulled my pillow over my eyes and drifted off to sleep with the lights on.

The next morning, after a restless night's sleep, I quickly got dressed and skipped breakfast, hoping to buy myself some extra time to find the agency, which, according to Daniel's notes, was just a short train ride away. There was just one problem: his note didn't tell me how to find the train station.

Dear God, don't let this adventure involve a cab ride, I prayed silently.

Luckily, as I entered the lobby, I spotted a tall, thin, attractive blonde who had a look that just screamed, "Model."

Please, please, please let her speak English.

"Excuse me." I tapped her gently on the shoulder. She turned and flashed a warm, welcoming smile.

"I'm supposed to go to the Visage Agency," I said. "Would you happen to know where that is?"

"Yes. I'm going there myself," she responded in a thick accent that sounded either Russian or Polish. "My name is JoAnna." She extended her hand. "And you are?"

"Kylie."

"You must be new," she said, looking me over. "American?"

"Yes, I just got in last night." Relief flooded me. It seemed like a direct answer to prayer to find someone who spoke English—and someone who knew where we were going.

"Would it be okay if I went with you?" I asked.

"Of course!" She smiled. "I should warn you, though—it's quite a jaunt."

She was right. It *was* a long walk—and every bit as adventurous as my cab ride had been the night before. The first thing I noticed was the wildlife. Scurrying along the telephone wires that traversed the narrow alleyways where we walked were the biggest rats I'd ever seen. *They must feed on the giant cockroaches,* I mused.

"Best not to look up," JoAnna cautioned, noting the horrified look on my face. *Or down,* I added silently, reflecting on the disgusting floor show in my apartment the night before.

I took her advice, focusing my eyes straight ahead, and silently repeated the mantra, *It's all going to be worth it someday. It's all going to be worth it someday.*

After arriving at the station and boarding the train that would take us to the agency, JoAnna and I settled into side-by-side seats. I took a deep breath to calm my nerves. *How did I go from the bright lights and applause of Fashion Week to a dingy, roach-infested apartment in Japan in less than a week?* I wondered, watching the Osaka cityscape whir past.

When we arrived at the agency, we were met by a small, friendly looking Asian man who seemed happy to see us.

"Welcome! You must be Kylie," he said. "My name is Hiro. I'll be taking you and the other models to your castings while you are here. I see you have already met JoAnna." He nodded at my new friend. "Did you have any difficulty getting here?"

"Not really." I tried not to think about the rats, the roaches, or the underhanded cabdriver who drove off with half my money.

"Good, good," he responded cheerfully. "Come, I will introduce you to some of the others."

In addition to JoAnna, there were four other girls. JoAnna and

Ella were both from Poland, two others were from Russia, and one was from Germany. JoAnna and Ella both spoke a little English, and they made an effort to reach out to me. With the other girls there was more of a language barrier, and they pretty much kept to themselves. I didn't take it personally. We all were aware that this stint in Japan was just a stepping-stone on the way to something bigger, and we weren't exactly there to make friends. Even without a language barrier, modeling tends to be a competitive, cutthroat business—not exactly the type of environment that fosters good-will and lifelong friendships.

Day in and day out, Hiro drove us to various castings around the city. I mostly modeled wedding gowns and prom dresses for print ads. The modeling itself was a lot of fun—I loved showing off the fancy lace gowns, delicate veils, and snazzy dresses for the camera. But each day was bookended with rats above and roaches below. And I missed my family terribly.

When my grandma finally arrived, I was so happy I could have burst. I'd been in Osaka for only three weeks, but it felt like three years. *Finally,* I thought, clinging to my grandma at the train station, *someone to talk to besides the cockroaches.*

With just a twin bed, a table, and two chairs, the apartment was a little small for two people, but I didn't mind. After spending so much time on my own, I was grateful to be around someone who knew me.

Even though I was getting excellent experience doing print ad work just about every day, the highlight of my stay in Osaka was getting to spend time with Grandma. Because money was tight, we weren't able to do much sightseeing, and most of our meals were peanut butter and jelly sandwiches, with the occasional splurge on a fifteen-dollar watermelon. But I hadn't spent this much quality time with my grandma since I was a little girl in Jackpot, and that trade-off was worth all the cockroach-infested apartments in the world.

When it was time to leave Osaka, I made one last trip to Visage to pick up my check. I had gone on castings and done jobs almost every day, and I'd literally done dozens of print ads, so based on what Daniel had told me, I was expecting a pretty hefty sum. When Hiro presented me with a check in the amount of $500, I was stunned.

Five hundred dollars? What happened to the thousands I was supposed to make? I wondered.

"Is this everything?" I asked Hiro. "I worked dozens of jobs."

Hiro looked at me calmly. "This is your salary minus our commission, Envy's percentage, rent for your apartment, your cell phone and food allowances, and other incidentals."

I stared at him. Just like in New York, I'd never actually seen the money I made, nor had I been told how much I'd earned for each job. Once again, I was at the mercy of the agency. And once again, I had a strong suspicion that I'd gotten the short end of the stick. Between the two months I'd spent in New York and the two months I'd worked in Japan, I had netted just over six dollars a day.

If my financial situation didn't turn around quickly, I was going to have a really hard time convincing my parents to let me continue on this path. I had worked too hard for too long with nothing to show for it. And I was already seventeen. That was practically middle-aged in this industry. If I was ever going to have a legitimate shot at the big time, something was going to have to change.

And soon.

Chapter 11

DESPERATE MEASURES

The human heart is the most deceitful of all things,
and desperately wicked.
Who really knows how bad it is?

JEREMIAH 17:9, NLT

"I REALLY THINK you should consider it, Kylie." Daniel had been trying for the past twenty minutes to convince me to take a modeling gig in Singapore.

"No." I was adamant. "I'm not going overseas again. You promised if I went to Japan, you'd find me another agency in New York."

"I know," he began, "but this Singapore job would be perfect for you. It's formal wear, and you did such a great job with that in Japan."

I held firm. "No. I'm already seventeen. I can't waste any more time building a portfolio overseas. I want to get back to Fashion Week. It's either New York or nothing."

Daniel sighed. He knew he wasn't going to win this battle.

"Okay." He reached for a folder on the edge of his desk. "I spoke with someone at Red Model Management last week. They've seen your work, and they're interested." For some reason, Daniel seemed hesitant.

I, on the other hand, was thrilled. This was a *much* better opportunity for me. *Why isn't he excited about this?* I wondered.

"There's just one thing," Daniel said. "You'll need a new comp card." He paused for a second. "Kylie, they want a signature topless shot."

I froze.

"All their models have one." He looked directly at me. "It's a nonnegotiable."

Now I understood. Daniel knew how upset I'd been about the Saran Wrap incident earlier this year. He knew this would be an issue for me. What he didn't know was how desperate I'd become.

I'm not even sure I realized it myself—until it was too late.

"Go ahead and book the shoot." I felt my heart pounding uncontrollably.

"Are you sure?" he asked.

I held my breath, my mind flashing back to all the topless shots I'd seen on the comp cards of the models in New York—models who had beat me out for one job after another while I was dodging cockroaches in Japan.

Suddenly, breaking into the silence, I heard someone reply with a voice that sounded eerily similar to mine, "Yes."

As I headed out to meet Mom, who was waiting in the car, I was struck by the fact that this was the first meeting with Envy that Mom hadn't been present for. On the one hand, I was grateful.

What Mom and Dad don't know won't hurt them, I reasoned. But I still strongly suspect that, had Mom been there that afternoon, I would have been packing my bags for Singapore by dinner.

It's funny how the enemy can find your weak spot and attack precisely there. I was in no position—emotionally or spiritually—to make such a loaded decision on my own. I was desperate. I was insecure. I was scared. And I was tired of agencies pushing me around. In other words, I was a prime candidate for attack. The enemy saw it and pounced. God provided me with not one, but two, opportunities to walk away—first when Daniel offered me the job in Singapore, and again when he gave me the option to refuse the signature shoot. Unfortunately, I was so desperate to keep my career on track, to get back to New York, and to make my mark in the modeling world that I didn't see what really was happening.

Deep down, I knew it was wrong—otherwise I wouldn't have spent so much time and energy trying to rationalize it.

It's not like I'd be the first person to pose topless, I told myself. Heidi, Tyra, Giselle, Alessandra—all the top models had the same "signature shot" in their portfolios. *Besides,* I reasoned, *I'll just make sure I position my hair and arms in such a way that my chest is covered. With the proper lighting and the right camera angle, it actually could look quite fashionable in my book.*

I wasn't mature enough to understand this at the time, but it wasn't simply a question of what you can or can't see in those types of photos. My sinful choice was rooted in something deeper: what the photos represented. I can only imagine how sad it made God to see my complete lack of honor and purity and respect, not only for myself, but also for my parents, for my future spouse, and most of all, for Him.

Had I been further along in my Christian walk and more

focused on serving God rather than myself, I might have seen that. But I still had a long way to go in my faith. In my mind, being a Christian meant that God loved me and that He wanted me to be happy, healthy, and successful. I'd been listening to CDs that taught me how to transform my mind, when I should have been immersing myself in the Bible so God could transform my heart through His Word. Up to that point, I'd been treating God like a genie in a lamp, making childish wishes and then waiting for Him to deliver.

But God didn't send His Son to die on the cross so that one day I could become a famous fashion model. He doesn't exist to serve me; I exist to serve Him. Now I know what I didn't know then—that what we love most informs our decisions. When our lives are centered on living wholly for the Lord, the decisions we make will reflect that centeredness. But when our lives are focused on our selfish desires, we make decisions that end up having painful consequences.

At that point in my life, my heart was set on the selfish desire of advancing my career and becoming a famous model. As I learned the hard way, my selfish decisions pulled me further and further away from God, slowly eating away at my closeness with Him. By choosing to pose in the photo shoot, I wasn't living for God; I was living for my idol.

But all these realizations still were years away. Right now it was time to pack.

It had come at a considerable price, but I had gotten my wish. I was headed back to New York.

As Mom always used to say, "Be careful what you wish for."

Chapter 12

THE PRICE OF SUCCESS

The Lord does not look at the things people
look at. People look at the outward appearance,
but the Lord looks at the heart.

1 SAMUEL 16:7

ONCE I ARRIVED in New York, I went straight to the apartment
Red Model Management had arranged for me. I was hoping that
since Red Model was bigger and more prestigious than VMM, this
apartment would be an improvement over the cramped, four-to-a-
room arrangement I'd been placed in the last time around.

So much for that dream, I thought as I stood on the street looking up at my new home. It was a dingy-looking building with
bars on the windows, located in a less-than-savory section of
Chinatown.

The air reeked of a combination of rotting fish and day-old garbage that had been piled on the curb. That and something else . . .

What is *that smell?* I wondered as I climbed the stairs to apartment 3C. I got my answer as soon as I opened the door. I was

greeted by a haze of white smoke that emanated from the general direction of a pencil-thin blonde sitting on a beat-up sofa, taking a hit off a joint.

"Hey," she said, nodding in my direction. "You must be the new girl."

"Yeah." I waved away the haze and stifled a small cough. "I'm Kylie."

"Nice to meet you," she said. "I'm Brittany." She was about my height but much, much thinner—I guessed somewhere around 110, maybe even less. She was very pretty, with a Farrah Fawcett–type haircut and striking blue eyes. "You can have that bedroom." She pointed off to the left.

"Okay, thanks." I tried not to stare at the joint in her hand.

"Does the weed smell bother you?" she asked, taking another hit.

"No," I lied. "It's fine, really."

"Cool." She smiled weakly. "Well, welcome aboard." And with that she disappeared into the other bedroom, leaving me in a cloud of smoke.

Anxious to get away from the haze, I went into my bedroom and started to unpack. Since it was just the two of us, I actually had space to put things away this time instead of living out of my suitcase. That was a definite plus, but I wasn't so sure about Brittany. The truth was, the pot did bother me—and not just because of the smell. I'd always steered clear of drugs, and this was new, uncomfortable territory for me.

That night I called my mom and asked her to start scanning craigslist for another apartment—preferably one in a nicer neighborhood with a non-weed-smoking roommate. Unfortunately, Mom wasn't able to find anything even close to my price range—

unless I wanted to commute from New Jersey or share a room with four other girls. It looked like it was time to start getting comfortable with the roommate I'd been given.

Based on what I'd seen so far, I had no expectations that Brittany and I would become as close as Breanna and I had been, but I figured I could at least try to be friendly to her. After all, as anyone in the modeling industry will tell you, looks can be deceiving.

For the first few weeks after I moved in, Brittany kept her distance. I tried to start up casual conversations while we did the dishes or watched TV, but she didn't seem to be much of a talker. She just worked, slept, jumped rope, and smoked the occasional joint. Then one night we were sitting across from each other in the kitchen, and I noticed her eyes were red and puffy, as though she'd been crying.

"Are you okay?" I asked.

She looked down and sniffed. "Yeah, I'm fine."

"Are you sure?" I prodded. When she didn't respond, I reached across the table and gently put my hand on her wrist. That's when the floodgates opened.

Between sobs, Brittany told me that when she first started modeling, she was in great shape—not too thin, just healthy. But then, when she was sixteen, her agency sent her to Paris. The clients there wouldn't book her unless she lost a substantial amount of weight. That was when the nasty cycle began, and she developed bulimia.

She paused and said, "Hang on a second—I'll be right back." Brittany went to her room, and when she returned, she had a few photos in her hand.

"This was me in Paris," she said.

I was shocked to see that the girl in the pictures was even thinner than the one in front of me.

I was stunned. How could anyone think Brittany was overweight? She practically was skin and bones. But this was only a fraction of her story.

Over the course of the evening, I learned that Brittany had been struggling with bulimia for years and that she'd been hospitalized for malnutrition more than once since she began her modeling career at the age of fourteen. She'd even lost a baby as a result of her eating disorder.

I had no idea what to say. I'd known other girls in the industry who had struggled with bulimia and anorexia, but this felt like a bigger issue than I was qualified to handle. And besides, what encouragement could I offer? I knew it was virtually impossible to achieve and maintain the near-skeletal figures the labels demanded without resorting to one extreme measure or another. I had no doubt that was how my old roommates from VMM were able to eat and drink their weight in complimentary food and liquor all night at the clubs and still be able to slide into their skinny jeans the next day.

Sadly, a lot of girls don't recognize how dangerous—and potentially deadly—eating disorders are. They can cause irreparable damage to the heart, liver, and kidneys, and they may lead to bone loss, hair loss, gum disease, tooth decay, gastrointestinal issues, digestive disorders, infertility, reproductive concerns, miscarriage, and a myriad of other health problems. Many of the models I was around viewed these disorders simply as a way to lose weight, and they believed they could start and stop at any time. They had no idea how quickly the disease can take over.

That's precisely what was happening to Brittany. She'd been

forcing herself to regurgitate her meals for so long that she no longer could keep food down—even if she wanted to.

"And I'm still too fat!" she sobbed, burying her face in her hands.

At five feet nine and 110 pounds, Brittany was about as far from fat as someone could get. But in an industry where a size 4 is considered obese, the word *fat* takes on a twisted new meaning.

I felt utterly helpless. I'd never seen anyone so deeply entrenched in an eating disorder. I could tell Brittany that she wasn't fat, that she looked beautiful and just right the way she was. But I knew it wouldn't do any good. She wouldn't believe me. That's the most insidious aspect of the disease. Eventually it warps the victim's perception to the point where she is incapable of seeing herself accurately. Girls who are so malnourished that they are dependent on feeding tubes to keep them alive, with barely enough muscle mass to stand on their own power, look in a mirror and see an obese individual staring back at them. The disease eats away at a person's sense of reality until nothing is left but a shadow of who she used to be.

This is a prime example of the enemy at his worst. And once he grabs hold, it's almost impossible to pull free.

After that night, I started spending more time with Brittany, doing my best to support and encourage her, helping her develop a more sensible diet and exercise plan, and—when she needed it—giving her a shoulder to cry on. As the weeks passed, Brittany started leveling out a bit. She was keeping her food down, she had booked a couple of solid jobs, and the cloud of depression seemed to be lifting. Then, right when I thought she'd finally turned the corner, everything fell apart with the single click of a mouse.

"Are they up yet?" I asked. We were waiting to see the photos from the lingerie campaign Brittany had just done. I was sure that she would look amazing and that this would be just the self-esteem boost she needed right now.

"I'm looking," Brittany said, searching online. "Here, I found them."

"Brittany! You look amazing!" And she really did. Brittany had been beautiful all along, but now that she'd filled out a bit, she looked absolutely stunning. Then, in the computer screen, I saw the reflection of Brittany's face. She wasn't smiling.

"I look huge!" she cried. "Look at my thighs!"

"No you don't," I responded. "You look fantastic. Brittany, just look . . ." But before I could finish, she pushed back her chair and stormed off to her bedroom, slamming the door behind her.

We'd come all this way, and now, with just one image on the screen, Brittany was right back where she'd started. Later that evening, in the silence of the apartment, I could hear the telltale signs of the vicious cycle starting all over again. The enemy had Brittany firmly in his grasp. And I was standing precariously close to his outstretched hands.

"Are these my clothes?" I asked, flipping through the outfits on the rack.

"No, yours are over there." One of the assistants pointed to a rack on the other side of the room.

"Thanks." I walked to the other rack and grabbed the only two outfits on it.

That's funny, I thought. *I could have sworn they told me I'd be modeling three outfits today.*

"Excuse me," I said, catching the attention of a passing intern. "I seem to be missing an outfit. Do you know where it might be?"

"Let me find out," she said. Then she called across the studio, "Hey, does anyone know where the rest of the big model's clothes are?"

The big model? I froze, mortified, as all eyes turned to me.

How can I be the big model? My mind was reeling. *I'm only a size 2.* Convinced I must have misunderstood, I started thumbing through the other girls' outfits to check the sizes. Sure enough, every garment on the rack was either a size 0 or a size 00.

I *was* the big model.

I was flabbergasted. Back in high school, I'd thought I was too skinny when I weighed 125. Now here I was, almost ten pounds lighter, and all of a sudden I was fat?

This is insane, I thought. *I weighed the same amount back in February, and I walked in seven shows during Fashion Week!* Embarrassed but resolved, I gathered my "enormous" size 2 outfits and skulked off to change. Fall Fashion Week castings started in two weeks, and I felt confident there were at least some designers out there who would be happy to have me walk in their shows again. I took a deep breath. It was going to take a lot more than one thoughtless comment from an intern to make me crack.

Two weeks later, Fashion Week castings were in full swing. Brittany and several of the other models I knew from Red Model were going out on two, sometimes three, castings a day, and I had yet to be invited to one. My agent kept sending me out for more test shoots, even though my portfolio already was full. When she called to tell me about yet another test shoot, I pushed her for an explanation.

"Why am I doing another test shoot when everyone else is going out on castings for Fashion Week?"

"Do you really want to know, Kylie?" She sounded exasperated. "It's because you are a fat pig right now. You are a cow, and I don't want any of our clients to see you this way!"

I felt like I'd been kicked in the gut.

Before I could catch my breath to respond, she continued, "Your thighs are too big. Your butt is too big. You're just . . . *big!*"

Now the tears were falling. This was the second time in two weeks someone had told me I was too big. And this time it wasn't some lowly intern. It was my own agent—the person who was supposed to believe in me and fight for me. More importantly, she was the one who arranged all my bookings. Without her help, I was finished.

"Okay," I managed to sputter. "I'll work on it." Before she could say anything more, I hung up, collapsed on my bed, and sobbed.

What would I do? I already was thinner than I'd ever been. I couldn't imagine losing any more weight, nor could I imagine *how* I was supposed to lose any more weight. I was already doing double my normal cardio, and I had all but eliminated carbs from my diet. What was left?

I got up from the bed, walked to the full-length mirror, and took a good, long look. *I think I look pretty good,* I reasoned. But then, just as I was about to turn away, the voices started echoing in my mind: *Where are the big model's clothes? You are a fat pig. Your thighs are too big. Your butt is too big. You're a cow.*

That's when something switched inside me. *I suppose I could stand to lose a little off my waist,* I thought, running my hands from my ribs down to my hips. *And my thighs.* I turned to the right, glanced over my left shoulder, and sighed. *And my butt.*

It's amazing the power a few words can have on a person. When spoken in kindness, they can fill you with hope and encouragement and make you feel as if you can conquer the world. But when they're spoken in ignorance or cruelty, they can fill you with shame and self-doubt. And in my case, they made me see pounds that weren't even there.

❦

When I checked in at Red Model one morning in November, I could tell my agent was not happy.

"Why don't you just go home, Kylie." Her voice had an air of weary condescension in it. "Get an early jump on the holidays, and work on yourself. See if you can shed a few pounds."

"How much do you think I need to lose?" I was hoping to hear four, maybe five.

She took a quick look at me, zeroing in on my midsection. "I'd like to see you drop at least two inches off your hips and two from your waist, and the rest should fall off along with that."

"Oh."

The agent stood from her desk and started toward the door, signaling that it was time for me to leave. "I'll see you after the first of the year," she said, forcing a smile. "Hopefully, a lot less of you."

I followed her to the door, hoping I could hold the tears back long enough to make it out of her office.

By the time I got to the elevator, the tears were starting to fall. I saw a crowd waiting, so I turned and headed for the stairs instead. It was several flights down, but I didn't care. I couldn't get out of that building—and New York—quickly enough.

❦

"Kylie, you look just fine," Mom reassured me. "You're a beautiful girl. You don't need to change a thing."

It was so good to be home.

"You don't understand, Mom. I'm too big. Nobody will hire me like this." I tried to draw her attention to the love handles and saddlebags that existed only in my mind.

She shook her head. "Honey, I just don't see it."

"It doesn't matter if you see it," I shot back. "*They* see it. And if I ever want to book another job, I have to drop at least ten pounds."

Mom sighed. "Well, if you insist on dieting, at least do it sensibly."

She had a point. That night I sat down and did a little math. I had about six weeks in which to lose ten pounds. I figured if I worked out at the gym every day; jogged every morning; cut out all sugars, bread, pasta, and dairy; and ate only lean meat and veggies, I could pull this off.

I was wrong. After four weeks of constantly working out and barely eating enough to keep myself conscious, I had lost only one pound. I looked up from the bathroom scale and screamed in frustration before collapsing on the tile floor in a heap.

Mom was at my side almost instantly.

"Kylie, honey, what's the matter?" She crouched down beside me and wrapped me in a giant hug.

"I still have nine pounds to go," I gasped between sobs. "I'm never going to lose this weight. I'm huge. I'll never get another modeling job again."

Mom had heard and had enough. "Kylie, stop this. You are not huge." With that, she pulled me to standing position, opened the vanity drawer, pulled out a tape measure, and wrapped it around her waist, hips, and thighs. Then she measured me.

"Look, Kylie," she said, pointing to the tape measure. "See for yourself. I'm only five feet three and wear a size 3 petite, and you are *still* skinnier than me. Honey, these people have you seeing things that aren't even there. You have to stop!"

But it was no use. By that point, I couldn't hear anything but the voices in my own head—and they were telling me that if I didn't find a way to drop nine pounds in the next two weeks, my modeling career would be over.

Willing to try anything, I decided to go on a seven-day pineapple cleanse. I got the idea from a book my grandma had picked up at a yard sale that claimed you could lose ten pounds in one week. The time frame was just what I needed, and besides, I loved fruit, so it seemed like the perfect solution. As I read the instructions, though, I started getting worried that the diet was too nutritionally unbalanced and potentially unhealthy.

Basically the diet consisted of eating nothing but pineapple, papaya, and watermelon and drinking liter upon liter of water for a full week. Since you are consuming so few calories, you do lose weight. However, because your body isn't getting a sufficient supply of protein, most of the weight you lose doesn't come from fat but from muscle tissue—and that's not good. In addition, because you aren't taking in the appropriate vitamins and amino acids, your immune system can become compromised, causing you to feel dizzy and weak and leaving you susceptible to illness. The ultimate red flag should have been the book's warning that this cleanse wasn't a good idea for individuals with hypoglycemia, which I had. But I didn't care. Desperate times called for desperate measures. And I was desperate.

By the end of the fourth day, I was so dizzy and fatigued that I barely could get off the couch. As my family enjoyed holiday fudge, cookies, and one scrumptious meal after another, I methodically ate my pineapple chunks, drank my water, and watched the scale. By the end of the week, I was completely drained, shaky, and most likely anemic, but the cleanse had worked. With a little less than a week to go, I had reached my goal: 108 pounds.

❧

As I rode up the elevator on my way to meet with my agent, my heart was pounding. *What if I'm still not thin enough?*

My mom barely could look at me without crying the last few days I was at home, and both my dad and Luke kept doing double takes when they saw me, as if they didn't recognize me. It was heartbreaking. But at that point the look of approval on my agent's face was more important to me than the expressions of concern on my family's.

When the elevator doors opened, I took a deep breath, stepped into the reception area, and almost immediately was greeted by my agent. The look on her face said it all.

"Wow, Kylie, is that you?" She looked slightly stunned. "You look amazing!"

"Thank you." I was so relieved.

It had been a miserable six weeks. I'd barely spent any time with my family over the holidays, and I still was feeling tired and a little dizzy, but my agent was happy. At that moment, that was the only thing that mattered.

"Come on in," she said, gesturing toward her office. "Let's start booking you some jobs."

Chapter 13

INVISIBLE

Turn to me and have mercy,
for I am alone and in deep distress.

PSALM 25:16, NLT

Now THAT I WAS DOWN to a near-skeletal 108 pounds, I was getting booked for one job after another. When the time came for Fashion Week castings the following month, I was right back in the thick of the action.

My obstacles weren't all behind me, though. Keeping my weight in check while still maintaining enough energy to race across Manhattan on foot and stand in line hour after hour for auditions was proving to be more of a challenge than I'd expected. There were days when I would stand outside, shivering in the cold alongside more than a hundred other girls, just to get one minute with the designer. And with barely an ounce of meat on my bones, it made for some especially long, cold, miserable days.

It might seem like standing in line for hours on end with dozens of other girls in the same profession, all of whom shared the same hopes, dreams, and fears, would create a sense of camaraderie. But in fact, the exact opposite was true. Rarely did anyone strike up a conversation, say hello, smile, or look up from their phone long enough even to make eye contact. And yet, as self-involved as everyone was, every once in a while, I'd look up in time to catch six or seven sets of eyes quickly turn away after sizing me up to determine whether I might be a threat. The insecurity was almost palpable.

To my horror, there were several designers who still felt I was too big to model their lines. *Seriously?* I was five feet ten, 108 pounds, a size 0, and I was *still* too big? Even so, I ended up being cast in five different shows. That was two fewer than the year before, but I had managed to catch the attention of designers from a few different brands, including Custo Barcelona and Malan Breton.

Fashion Week went off much the same as it had the year before, complete with celebrity sightings, paparazzi, and of course, all the backstage chaos. Like the last year, I loved every minute I spent on the runway, showing off the newest fashions and making both the clients and my agent proud. And like the last year, I tolerated yet despised the backstage melodrama and cattiness. Still, I had walked in my second New York Fashion Week—an accomplishment that would have meant worlds more to me had it not been for one thing. There was nobody from my family there to share the experience with me. Dad was too busy with his new business to make the trip, and Mom had to be home to take Luke to all of his sporting events, so a weeklong visit to New York would have been impossible for either of them.

Poor Luke, I lamented. I'd been so preoccupied with losing those ten wretched pounds over Christmas that I'd barely spent any time with him. *Who knows when I might get to see him again?* He was growing up fast, and I'd never felt so far away.

I missed my entire family. Mom. Dad. Luke. Grandma. Papa. Everyone.

I'd never imagined I could feel so isolated and alone in a city of eight million people.

For the next several weeks, my life consisted of little more than working, exercising, and sleeping. Thanks to a good showing in Fashion Week, my agent was busy booking jobs for me. Finally, after three and a half years, I legitimately could say that I was a "working model."

I loved the work. Whether it was the encouragement and accolades I received from the photographers, the beautiful clothes, or mastering the mechanics of turning my head and body to just the right angle for the perfect shot, there was something about modeling—especially in front of the camera—that appealed to me. As soon as the shoots were over, though, and the attention was gone, I felt utterly empty and alone. I always had plenty of invitations to go clubbing with the other models, but it just wasn't my scene. I didn't smoke or drink, and the idea of grinding up against a bunch of total strangers on a packed dance floor until three in the morning was not my idea of a good time. I was much more comfortable hanging out at the apartment and talking to Mom on the phone.

So while the other models were out dancing the night away, I spent most of my evenings going for long walks by myself. That's when I realized there were actually a lot of lonely people in New York. Not that I wasn't aware of them before. In fact, I passed dozens of them on my way to and from work every day. I'd just never paid much attention to them. But one night, with no place to go and nobody to talk to, I felt compelled to stop and say hello to one of the countless homeless people who lived alone and unnoticed on the streets of New York.

"Hello," I said tentatively, squatting down in front of an elderly man leaning against a trash can. He looked up, startled, and stared back at me with intense blue eyes.

"My name's Kylie," I continued, putting out my hand.

He reached out a dirty, calloused hand and reluctantly shook mine. When I smiled at him, he cautiously revealed a grin that was in need of some good dental work.

"Why are you talking to me?" He clutched the collar of his worn jacket, understandably leery of my motives.

"Because I don't have anyone to talk to," I replied honestly. "And besides, you look like you could use a friend."

"I have friends," he mumbled defensively, pointing his chin in the direction of several other homeless people down the street. "But I'll talk to you if you want."

"Thank you." I sat down cross-legged in front of him. "What's your name?" I asked. And so our conversation began.

That was the day I stopped *looking* at the homeless people in New York City and actually began *seeing* them, not as a problem to be ignored or feared or even pitied, but for exactly who they were—real people with real feelings, who, just like the rest of us, had made their share of mistakes. God knew I had made plenty of my own mistakes in the past couple of years. Walking the streets of New York gave me a much-needed fresh perspective on life. Here were people who were starving—not because they were desperate to fit into a size 00 gown so they could walk in a silly fashion show, but because they simply couldn't afford to eat.

My priorities had become seriously out of whack. I'd been spending too much time surrounded by vain, superficial people who obsessed about nothing but their looks, and somewhere along the way, I'd become just like them. The people I met on the streets couldn't have cared less what size I wore, what my measurements were, how much I weighed, or which designers I had walked for in fashion shows. All they saw when they looked at me was someone who cared enough to spend some time getting to know them, who treated them to a sandwich or a cup of soup, and who made them smile and feel like human beings again—if only for a little while. Every time I stopped to speak with one of them, that cold, lonely city seemed a little bit warmer, a little bit friendlier.

I'm always amazed at how God puts lessons in my path just when I need them most. I desperately needed that lesson in priorities. And I desperately needed the lesson He had for me next: a reminder of the importance of family.

I missed my family terribly. I'd been given a chance to spend six weeks of quality time with them over Christmas, and I'd squandered it obsessing over my weight.

Thankfully, God is patient with us, not to mention generous. He was about to give me another chance. My eighteenth birthday was right around the corner, and that year's gift couldn't have been a better cure for what was dragging me down. And it couldn't have come at a better time.

Chapter 14

UNEXPECTED BLESSINGS

From the fullness of his grace we have all
received one blessing after another.

JOHN 1:16

I DIDN'T REALIZE how desperately I'd needed to get away from New
York and the whole modeling scene until I found myself seated at a
beautiful seaside restaurant in Cancún, sharing a delicious seafood
dinner with my parents. We never would have been able to afford
a trip like this, but Dad's new company was big on perks, and this
was his reward for a successful year—a weeklong executive retreat
for two at a gorgeous resort in sunny Cancún. Since the retreat
happened to coincide with my eighteenth birthday, Mom and
Dad paid for me to join them as a special gift—and was it ever.

My priorities had gotten completely out of whack over the
past few months, and I needed some time away to slow down and
refocus. The many hours I'd spent visiting with the homeless in
New York made me realize how trivial and superficial my life had

become. Interestingly, those connections also reminded me how much I missed being with my family. The part of this trip I was looking forward to most—even more than the tropical location or the opportunity to relax—was the chance to remember who I was. I knew that one of the keys to doing that would be reconnecting with my parents. So far, things were off to an excellent start.

It was a lovely evening. Sitting outside with a magnificent view of the ocean and a faint breeze blowing through my hair, I thought back to my last night of camp at Huntington Beach. It had been less than two years since I'd tossed that piece of wood into the fire and committed my life to Christ, but it seemed like a lifetime ago. I had drifted far from God since leaving home, and I was feeling the loss. I had become self-absorbed, spending an inordinate amount of time worrying about my looks, my weight, and my career. The time I used to devote to reading my Bible was now spent flipping through the pages of fashion magazines and comparing myself to the models inside. I had stopped seeing myself through God's eyes and instead was basing my self-worth on the opinions of agents, stylists, and designers who saw me as nothing more than a glorified clothes hanger.

I missed going to church with my mom on Sundays, attending youth group meetings, and studying the Bible with our small group leader. I especially missed the way it felt to be around my Christian friends. There was no cattiness or competition with them—just kindness and openness. When they looked at me, they didn't see a nameless, faceless mannequin who could show off their latest designs; they saw someone they genuinely loved and cared about. They saw *me*—Kylie, the person. I missed that. And more than anything, I missed my relationship with God. I was tired of flailing around trying to do life on my own, like a leaf being tossed around in the wind. I missed being grounded and safe and secure, with the assurance that God was the One in control of my life.

I knew the other key to getting back to the core of who I was—the most important one, at that. While I was in Cancún, I wanted to renew my relationship with God.

∽∾

"It's a shame Luke couldn't be here, isn't it?" Mom mused wistfully, looking out at the water. "He would have loved to see the ocean." But before I could answer her, something—or rather, *someone*—caught my eye.

Sitting directly across from me, two tables away, was the most handsome man I had ever seen in my life. He had dark eyes and dark hair and was wearing a sharp-looking dress shirt—definitely younger and more casual than the smattering of middle-aged businessmen from my dad's company who were dining at the restaurant that evening.

The man looked up and smiled at me, and I quickly averted my eyes to my plate, feeling a flood of warmth rush into my cheeks. I glanced up again, and as our eyes met for the second time, I felt my mouth form into a smile—seemingly without my permission.

"Did you hear me, Kylie?" Mom asked, breaking the spell.

"Oh, sorry. What was that?"

Mom and Dad continued talking, but their voices faded into the background as I became increasingly entranced by the mysterious stranger across the way. Every time I looked in his direction, his face lit up in a sweet, innocent smile. Our glances became more and more frequent as the meal progressed, and by the time dessert was served, it felt as though we were the only two people in the restaurant.

"Kylie?" Mom was looking at me, obviously waiting for a reply. "What do you think?"

Uh-oh. I'd been so lost in my own thoughts, I had no idea what Mom was just talking about. "I'll be back in a minute," I quickly covered. "I need to use the restroom."

It was the perfect escape. And as an added bonus, the ladies' room was located just beyond the mystery man's table, meaning I'd have to walk right past him.

As I passed by, I shot him a quick smile, hoping he'd stand and introduce himself. Instead, he simply returned the smile and nodded at me.

When I went by again on my way back to our table, I glanced over my shoulder and caught his gaze just as he was reaching for his water glass. His hand froze in midair, and he broke into a huge grin, blushing ever so slightly.

"Ready to call it a night, Kylie?" My dad stood from the table. "We have a big day ahead of us tomorrow."

"Yep." I tried to sound as enthusiastic as possible. After all, we did have a big day planned. The three of us were going snorkeling together, which felt like a big deal since we hadn't done anything like that in years. When I'd sat down for dinner that evening, our adventure was at the forefront of my mind. Now, however, all I could think about was the mysterious stranger—and whether I would ever see him again.

That night, before drifting off to sleep, I did something I hadn't done in far too long. I prayed.

God, thank You for giving me this time with my parents. I've missed them so much, and I want us to be close again. Thank You for watching over me in New York—for keeping me safe and for reminding me what really matters. I know I still have a lot to learn. Please help me to make the right decisions, and help me to seek Your plans for my life. Amen.

For a moment, I considered asking God about the mysterious stranger I'd seen at dinner, but somehow it didn't feel right. I couldn't have known then that he was part of God's plan all along.

❧

"This is going to be amazing," I told my parents as we waited for the tour bus that would take us to the snorkeling site. I'd always wanted to go snorkeling, and the fact that I was experiencing this for the first time with my parents was the best birthday present I could have imagined. "This is going to be the best day ever!" I gushed. If someone had told me it was about to get even better, I'm not sure I would have believed it.

Just as the bus pulled up to the curb, there he was—the mysterious man from dinner the night before. Seeing him in such close proximity actually took my breath away, and I gasped.

"What is it, Kylie?" my mom asked.

"Nothing." I smiled nervously. "I'm just really excited." *Now, more than ever.*

When we boarded the bus, the dark-eyed man sat a few rows in front of us. My thoughts were racing. *What are the odds he would be here? And what is it about this guy that makes my heart rate do double time?*

The bus ride went by in a blur of speculation. I didn't even realize we'd stopped until I heard the guide announce, "Here we are! From here you'll take ATVs down to the snorkel site."

"Wow!" my dad exclaimed. "How long has it been since we've gone on ATVs together, Ky?"

"Too long." I smiled at him. It *had* been ages. Mystery man or not, this was going to be a fantastic day.

We each picked out an ATV and made our way down the trail to the beach. I was having the time of my life. I saw my dad racing ahead of me, and I was just about to gun the engine to try to overtake him when I noticed that he was riding right next to my mystery man. The two of them were talking and laughing as if they'd known each other for ages. Anxious to hear what they were saying, I pulled a little closer, but before I could make anything out, we rounded a corner and the beach came into full view.

By the time I parked my ATV, the stranger had vanished from sight. I saw my dad sorting through the pile of snorkels and fins, so I headed his way.

"Here you go," he said, handing me a set of swim fins and then turning to put on his gear. I was just about to ask him who the guy was when I heard a voice behind me say, "Follow me."

I spun around, and there he was—holding a snorkeling mask in one hand and offering the other one out to me. He had the same sweet smile on his face that he'd had last night, and once again, as soon as our eyes met, everything else around me disappeared.

"Come on. Follow me," he repeated. There was a shyness about him mixed with a sense of assurance. Instantly I was overcome with the most extraordinary sensation. I didn't even know this man's name, yet somehow I trusted him completely. Without thinking, I reached out and took his hand. I've been following him ever since.

We spent the entire afternoon exploring the ocean together— swimming alongside tropical fish and taking in the beauty of the coral. As enchanting as the ocean was that afternoon, I was even more mesmerized by the extraordinary man with whom I was sharing this adventure.

Once we were back on land, though, I suddenly found myself racked with nerves. Being with him when our faces were underwater was one thing. But back in the real world, I didn't know what to say to this person I barely knew but felt such a powerful tug toward. Somehow I managed to sputter out a quick thank-you and then hurried off to meet my mom, who was relaxing on the beach.

"Did you have a nice time, honey?" Mom smiled at me, shielding her eyes from the sun. I was grateful she couldn't see very well because I was sure I was blushing again.

"Yeah, it was great," I stammered nervously, casting a quick glance back to see if I could still see. . . . *Oh, shoot. I forgot to ask his name!*

"I see you ditched me for Mike." Dad plopped down next to Mom on the sand and pulled off his fins. "He's a great guy. I've worked with him a few times in the past."

Mike! So that was his name. And he worked with my dad.

"Yeah," I said cautiously. "He seems like a really nice guy." I turned to scan the waterline again, but Mike was nowhere to be found.

"Come on," my dad announced, pulling my mom to a standing position. "I'm starved. Let's head back to the hotel and get something to eat."

Back at the hotel, I was kicking myself for not getting to know Mike better. *What if I never see him again? I didn't even tell him my name! Oh, God, what am I going to do?*

Fortunately, God had everything under control.

❧

"I'll have the crab legs, please," I told the waiter. I tried to appreciate the moment, but I couldn't hide the dejection in my voice. Even a scrumptious seafood dinner at one of the resort's five-star restaurants couldn't lift my mood that night. All I could think about was Mike and how I'd probably never see him again.

"I heard that Spencer and some of the other guys from work are going to explore Cancún tonight," Dad said. "Would you like to go, Kylie?"

Some of the other guys, I thought. *Maybe Mike will be there!* It was a bit of a long shot, but I was willing to take it.

"Can we?" I asked Dad.

"If they haven't left before we finish our dinner." He took another bite of his steak. "I don't see why not."

I ate so quickly I barely swallowed. "Okay, I'm done." I set down my napkin.

But Mom and Dad didn't seem to sense the urgency of the situation.

"Come on," I urged. "If we don't hurry, we might miss them!"

"Hey, calm down," Mom said. "Why do you want to go so much anyway? They'll probably just end up at a club somewhere, and you hate clubs."

I slumped in my chair, convinced Mom and Dad would never finish in time. After what seemed like an eternity, Dad called for the check, and we headed back to the hotel. When we entered the lobby, I couldn't believe my eyes—there was Mike, standing with an older gentleman I didn't recognize. As if in answer to my prayer, Dad walked right over and started talking to him.

"Mike, good to see you again." Then Dad turned to Mom.

"This is my wife, Yolanda. And of course, you've met my daughter, Kylie," he said, gesturing to me.

"Hi, Kylie." Mike smiled and reached to take my hand. "It's nice to meet you—formally." I took his hand and didn't want to let go. "This is my dad, Richard," he continued, nodding at the man standing with him. "He'd never been to Cancún before, so I brought him as my guest."

As we were talking, my dad's business partner, Spencer, arrived and asked if we were ready to go. Mike looked at me, and I could see in his eyes that he was hoping we'd go too. I silently prayed that Dad would say yes.

"Sure," Dad told Spencer.

It was all I could do to keep from jumping up and down. I'd never felt this way before—not about Lance, and certainly not about Jake. In fact, I hadn't really gotten involved in the dating scene since I left Las Vegas. I was too busy with modeling, and most of the guys I'd met in the industry weren't the kind of guys I wanted to date anyway. Most were either looking for a piece of eye candy to help promote their clubs or were so self-involved there really wasn't room for anyone else.

Besides, after the fiasco with Jake, I knew that when I did date again, I would only go out with another Christian, like Lance. Though our relationship didn't last all that long, I appreciated that we shared the common bond of our faith. Lance treated me with honor and respect, and he genuinely wanted to help me grow in my relationship with the Lord. That was the kind of guy I was looking for. Now, there was one big question: What kind of guy was Mike?

As Mom had predicted, we did end up at a club, but it wasn't anything like the club scene in New York, with techno music blaring and people grinding all over each other. This place was actually kind of nice. They played a lot of '80s music, which my parents used to listen to when I was growing up, and Mike and I ended up sitting at a table with my dad and Spencer, talking and laughing and getting to know each other.

"You really like these old songs?" he asked, surprised that I knew all the words.

"Yeah," I said. I couldn't get over how comfortable it was to talk to Mike. "My parents always played this kind of music when I was little. It's my favorite."

"Wow! Mine, too!" Mike grinned at me.

As the evening wore on, Mike and I discovered that we had a lot more in common than just music. Like me, he enjoyed hunting, camping, and spending time outdoors. He also shared my love for riding ATVs, fishing, and playing basketball. I could have talked to him all night. Then, in the middle of our conversation, my dad pulled Mike aside and told him that if he wanted to, he could ask me to dance. Mike was surprised.

"Really?" he exclaimed. "It's okay with you if I dance with your daughter?"

"Of course," Dad responded, shooting me a tender glance. "She's been living on her own in New York for a while now. I think she's old enough to share a dance with you."

I couldn't believe my ears. The same man who had always been so protective of me and had forbidden me to date throughout most of my teenage years was setting me up for a dance.

As we stepped onto the dance floor, Mike told me how happy he was that he'd met me. We danced to one song after another. I wasn't usually the dancing type, especially in public, but in that moment, it seemed just right. In fact, that night *everything* seemed just right.

When I got back to my hotel room, I couldn't stop smiling.

Then I remembered the promise I'd made to myself. *Mike seems so perfect for me,* I thought. *But what if he isn't a Christian?* I hadn't even thought to ask him. My heart sank. *If he isn't,* I thought, *it would be a deal breaker for sure.*

My head swimming, I climbed into bed and uttered a silent prayer before drifting off to sleep. *Lord, I've never felt this way before. Please show me if he's a believer.*

The very next night I got my answer.

A large group of people from Dad's company decided to go into town and get fish tacos. When we arrived at the restaurant, I sat flanked by Mike and his dad on one side and my parents on the other. Just as we were about to eat, Mike silenced the group and said, "Let's bless the food before we start eating."

He didn't hesitate before launching into a prayer. "Dear Lord, thank You for this time we all have together and for this food we are about to eat. I pray that You will keep us safe as we are away from our homes and that we will honor You in our business. Amen."

A huge smile lit up my face. "You're a Christian!" I blurted out.

"Yes, I am," Mike said. "All my life. Are you?"

"Yes!" I exclaimed. "And I'm glad you are, too, or that would have been it!" We both laughed, and he gave me a quick hug. I couldn't get over how natural—how right—it felt being there with Mike. It was as though we'd known each other our entire lives. Sitting there with Mike, his father, and my parents, I felt indescribably content and utterly loved. There was no doubt in my mind: this kind of feeling could only come from God.

After we left the restaurant, Mike asked my dad if he could take a walk with me on the beach. Mom and Dad looked at each other and then at Mike and me. Finally Dad smiled. "Sure," he told Mike.

I was a little surprised that Dad allowed this, but later he told me that he knew enough about Mike's character from work and from what he'd seen over the past two days to trust him.

As we headed toward the beach, Mike took my hand, and I felt so happy I thought my heart would burst. He was sweet and funny and comfortable in his own skin—the exact opposite of the men I'd met in New York. We picked up our conversation right where we'd left off the night before, and we discovered that we had even more things in common. We both were crazy about board games and coffee ice cream, and we both dreamed of living on a ranch someday.

"A true country girl who loves the Lord," he said, smiling at me. "Just my type."

Then we sat down in the sand and shared our stories of how we came to know the Lord. I had told only a handful of people about my shameful history with Jake, but that night I told Mike everything. True to his character, he wasn't judgmental; instead, he showed me grace and understanding. As it turned out, Mike had a somewhat checkered romantic past himself. He had been married for two and a half years and had a one-year-old son, Noah. He filed for divorce when he found out his wife had committed adultery shortly after Noah was born.

This was a lot to wrap my head around. I'd never dated someone who had been through a divorce before, let alone someone who had kids. Yet I felt an inexplicable peace about it all. A peace I knew could only have come from God.

After we talked for more than an hour, Mike walked me back to my room. When we reached the door, he softly tucked a strand of hair behind my ear. "Some of my business partners are getting together for a Bible study on the beach tomorrow morning," he said. "Would you like to join me?"

"It's a date," I replied with a smile.

He smiled back. "Good night, gorgeous." Then he kissed me gently on the forehead and walked away.

Thank You, God. Thank You so much.

The next morning I woke up, grabbed my Bible, and ran to meet Mike on the beach. The group started out with a prayer and then dug into the Word. Mike's dad was there, and to my surprise, he was the one leading the study. I hadn't been involved in any Bible studies or small groups in New York, and suddenly I realized how much I'd missed discussing God's Word with other people. Mike and his dad were obviously mature Christians, and it was encouraging to see how deep and genuine their faith was. This was exactly the kind of community I'd been missing in New York.

Wow, Lord, You really are orchestrating all of this, aren't You?

On our final night in Cancún, the company held a farewell dinner for all the business associates, and I invited Mike to join my parents and me at our table. I had gotten to know Mike's dad a bit at the Bible study that morning, and I wanted my parents to become more acquainted with Mike, too. By the end of the evening, I think my parents were almost as impressed with Mike as I was. After dinner Mike asked me if I wanted to take another walk under the stars, and of course, I obliged.

We walked and talked and finally sat on the sand to enjoy the rhythmic pounding of the waves. The breeze was picking up and I was a little cold, so Mike held me close. I didn't have to say anything; he just instinctively knew what I needed.

"You know what's weird?" Mike asked.

"What?"

"I've only known you for a couple of days, but I feel like

something really special is happening. I can't explain it, but nothing has ever felt so right."

"I feel the same way." I was at once delighted and relieved that I wasn't the only one feeling this way.

We talked for hours, and then I finally got up the nerve to ask the inevitable question: "When will we see each other again?" My heart stood still as I waited for his answer. I couldn't bear the thought of him going back to his home in LA.

"Well," he said thoughtfully, "where will you be next week? In New York?"

"No," I responded. "I'm going to be in Vegas, at my parents' house."

"You're kidding," Mike shot back. "I'm going to be in Las Vegas with my dad for a real estate seminar next week!"

"No way!" I was sure *he* was kidding. "You're making that up, right? There's no way you could have planned a trip to Las Vegas before you even met me."

"What can I say, Ky? God is good!" He pulled me into a hug.

Then he turned serious. "Can I take you out on an official date when I'm in town?"

"I would love that." I smiled. *God is good,* I marveled.

I practically floated up to my hotel room that night, and after crawling into bed, I prayed a simple yet genuine prayer. *Thank You, God, for unexpected blessings.*

Chapter 15

FINALLY, THE FAIRY TALE

All glory to God, who is able, through his
mighty power at work within us, to accomplish
infinitely more than we might ask or think.

EPHESIANS 3:20, NLT

I COULD HARDLY WAIT for Mike to arrive in Las Vegas. Although
we'd known each other only a week and we'd been apart just a few
days, I could barely stand being without him. As driven and consumed as I'd been with my career over the past several months, it all
seemed to fade into the background now that I'd met Mike Bisutti.

When I saw his number come up on my phone, my heart
practically leaped into my throat.

"Where are you?" I asked, not even trying to mask my anticipation.

"I'm about five minutes out from your house," he said. "I can't
wait to see you."

When Mike pulled into our driveway, I literally ran out to meet
him. After he said hello to my mom and dad and met Luke, Mike

and I went on our first official date—a lovely dinner for two at P.F. Chang's. Mike was the perfect gentleman—opening doors for me, pulling out my chair, always making sure I was comfortable. This was new territory for me, and I loved every minute of it.

Later that evening, we went back to my parents' house and played board games with my parents and brother. When I saw Mike interacting with my family—especially my dad—I wondered if he was too good to be true. The two of them got along like old friends.

Who is this guy? I wondered as I stared across the table at Mike, who was laughing at a corny joke my dad had just told. *I mean, who plans a first date that includes the girl's family?*

At that moment Mike turned and looked right at me, and I absolutely melted. *The right kind,* I concluded.

After we finished playing games, my parents excused themselves, and Mike and I went outside to look at the stars. He kissed my forehead, and then, just as I'd been dreaming, he took my face in his hands and slowly pulled me in for our first kiss.

"I'm crazy about you," Mike said, gazing at me intensely. "I can't explain it. I just know I've never felt like this before."

He didn't have to explain it. I knew exactly how he felt.

I remember asking my grandma, when I was little, how she knew my grandpa was the perfect man for her. She simply smiled and said, "Kylie, honey, when you know, you know." Well, now I knew.

After Mike left, I came back into the house, practically glowing with joy. Mom grinned. "So . . . did you have a nice evening?"

"Mom," I said with conviction. "I'm going to marry that man someday."

She rolled her eyes, but I saw the corners of her mouth tilting up in a smile.

※

Not only was I falling for Mike, but the rest of my family was too. That week we spent as much time together as possible, playing board games, pinochle, and even a little basketball.

"You may have beaten me at Monopoly," Mike teased, "but you're not going to beat me in basketball. How about a little two on two? Your mom and me against you and your dad?"

"I don't know." Dad winked at me. "Kylie and I make a pretty great team, don't we, Ky?"

"Yep," I answered, remembering the old days when Dad and I used to play together every weekend. "We sure do."

I don't know how he did it, but somehow Mike was managing to bring my family together, helping us re-create the wonderful family times we'd had in Jackpot.

This has to be God, I thought.

Not only had the Lord brought me the love of my life, but after years of distance, He'd brought my dad back too. This was quickly becoming one of the most wonderful weeks of my life. I didn't want it to end.

"So, when are you going back to New York?" Mike asked. It was his last night in Las Vegas, and considering we lived on opposite coasts, we needed to know where our relationship was headed.

The funny thing was, I hadn't given New York—or modeling, for that matter—a single thought since Mike and I had met. And though it surprised me to admit it, I really didn't miss that world one bit. Being with Mike and my family had brought me more joy and a deeper sense of fulfillment than I could have achieved walking in a thousand Fashion Weeks. And frankly, the thought of going back to that dingy apartment and breathing in the sickening stench of Brittany's weed made my stomach turn.

Why on earth would I go back to New York when everything I've ever wanted is right here?

I took a deep breath, looked at Mike, and said, "I don't think I'm going back. At least, not anytime soon."

His eyebrows raised in surprise.

"I know it sounds crazy," I said, "but I really believe the Lord is orchestrating something amazing in my life right now. And to tell you the truth, things aren't really working out with my room-mate in New York."

I thought back to how conflicted I'd felt before the Cancún trip. Without consciously thinking through my reasons, I'd packed up a lot of my things before I left. It was almost as if the Lord was preparing me for what He knew was going to happen in Cancún. I marveled at how seamlessly God had been working in the background.

"The timing of it all feels so . . . perfect," I said.

"God does work in amazing ways." Mike flashed me his heart-melting smile.

"Here's the thing," I whispered. "Until I met you, my biggest dream was to become a famous model. But now . . ." I paused to collect my thoughts. "I'm going to be honest, Mike. I'm falling in love with you."

"Well, that's good," he said sweetly. "Because I'm falling in love with you, too."

The decision was final. I was not going back to New York.

∼∞∽

Brittany was less than ecstatic about my decision, since she now was lacking a roommate—not to mention my share of the rent. The people at Red weren't too pleased either. After all, between Fashion Week and the print jobs I had gotten, they were making some pretty good money off me. My agent in Vegas, on the other hand, was thrilled to have me available for the local market again.

My plan was to move back in with my parents until I could scrape together enough money to get an apartment near Mike in LA. With the experience I'd gained in New York, I was confident I could sign with a small modeling agency in Los Angeles that would find me enough local work to stay afloat while Mike and I got to know each other better. In my mind, it was a win-win situation. My parents, however, weren't quite as sold on my plan.

"You know we like him, Kylie," Mom explained. "But don't you think you're moving a little fast? I mean, you've only known Mike a few weeks."

"Oh, Mom, you worry too much," I said. "Mike and I have already had 'the relationship talk,' and we've agreed to focus on our relationship with each other and on our relationship with Christ." I grabbed her hand. "He's the one, Mom. I know it."

Mom still seemed skeptical, but she had to admit that not only was I happier than I'd been in years, I also was healthier. All the dining out Mike had been treating me to had gotten me up to a more respectable weight. And after all I'd put Mom through over Christmas, I think she was willing to give me the benefit of the doubt. Beyond that, she really liked Mike, and she respected how genuine he was about his faith. The fact that Dad absolutely adored Mike didn't hurt either. Things may have been moving quickly, but compared to where I'd been six months ago, she couldn't deny that my life was clearly heading in the right direction. And things were about to start moving even more quickly.

The next weekend Mike flew out from LA for a visit.

"Welcome home!" I gushed, rushing outside to greet him. Even though it technically was my home, not his, ever since I'd met Mike I felt as though "home" was wherever the two of us happened to be at the moment. It was the place I wanted most, the place I belonged.

"Hey, sweetie." Mike wrapped me in a huge hug. "I've missed you."

"Me, too," I said, walking him to the house.

"I want to do something really special today, okay?" Mike said.

I nodded, smiling. I didn't care what we did as long as we were together. After we dropped Mike's things off at my parents' house, we hopped in his car and headed for the mall. As we walked along hand in hand, I had a feeling he was up to something, but I wasn't sure what. Then, to my surprise, we stopped in front of a jewelry store.

"Kylie, I know we've only known each other for a short time," he said. "But I am 100 percent sure I want to be with you for the rest of my life."

My heart was pounding right out of my chest. "I feel the exact same way."

He looked straight into my eyes. "I want to make it official with promise rings."

"Oh, Mike, I'd love that!" I flung my arms around his neck in a tight hug. "And I love you."

"I love you, too," he whispered. The moment was perfect. Mike was perfect. Everything was perfect.

We chose matching silver bands, which we wore on our right ring fingers as a reminder of our commitment to each other and as a celebration of the life we planned to share. True, we'd known each other only a month, but it had been the best thirty days of my life. I had found my soul mate—a person who loved God and who adored me and my family. He was everything I could have wanted.

The next day I planned a special date for Mike and me, starting with a trip to Jamba Juice and an outing to a local park. I spread out the blanket I'd packed, and then I plopped down and took out my Bible.

"I thought we could start our day together by reading the Word," I said. "Like we did in Cancún with your dad."

Mike sat beside me, took my hand, and prayed—for us, for our day together, and for the many days we hoped to share together down the road. I don't know if it was the summer sunshine, God's sovereignty, or simply being this close to the man I loved, but I couldn't remember ever feeling so happy, so safe, and so loved as I did in that moment.

After that I took Mike to play miniature golf, followed by lunch at In-N-Out Burger, where I shocked him by putting away a 3x3 Animal Style with cheese fries.

"Wow!" he exclaimed. "For someone your size, you sure know how to eat."

He was right—I *did* love to eat. That was one of the hardest parts about modeling for me—having to watch my diet like a hawk, when what I really wanted was to tear into a deep-dish Meat Lover's pizza and a pint of Häagen-Dazs. Being with Mike gave me the freedom to be myself instead of worrying about being the perfect size 0 for my agency. For dessert, I treated Mike to a couple of Double Doozie cookies at the mall. It was a simple day, but a special one. Special for me because I'd spent it with Mike. Special for him because it was the first time anyone had ever planned an entire day just for him.

"Seriously, Kylie." Mike took my hand. "I'm overwhelmed. Nobody has ever made me feel as special as you did today."

"Really?" I was shocked that I was the first woman to plan a date for such a wonderful man. "Well, the day isn't over yet."

From there, I took Mike to a place where we made our own clay coffee mugs. Mike made one that said, "Ky has my heart in her hands." Mine said, "Mike, you are the man of my dreams." We have those coffee cups to this day. I still do, and he still is.

"Last but not least," I teased, "coffee ice cream from Häagen-Dazs."

"Yes!" Mike said, smiling. "You remembered."

"Of course!" I poked him gently in the ribs. "I don't think I'll forget anything you said to me that first night."

As we sat together eating our ice cream, laughing, and simply enjoying each other's company, it was the first time I'd ever looked at a guy and thought, *You know, I could see myself growing old with him.*

One of the things I loved most about Mike was that he knew absolutely nothing about the modeling industry. Once, when we were in LA and sitting at our gate at the airport, I glanced up from what I was reading just in time to see Heidi Klum walking by, flanked by photographers.

"Mike! Look! It's Heidi Klum," I whispered in his ear, staring after her in amazement.

"Who's Heidi Klum?"

"*Who's Heidi Klum?* How can you not know that?" I protested. "She's one of the most famous models of all time!"

"Oh." He didn't seem overly impressed. "Are you going to say hello?"

"No, I'm not going to say hello!" I laughed. "She has no idea who I am."

In Mike's mind, she was a model and I was a model, so surely we knew each other.

Mike wasn't mesmerized by Heidi Klum, and he wasn't enchanted with me because I was a model, either. He loved me for me—not for how I looked, how much I weighed, what runways I'd walked, or what magazines I'd appeared in. Truth be told, he was far more impressed with the fact that I hunted, that I could gut a deer by myself, and that I wasn't afraid to get my hands dirty. There was no question about it: the more I discovered about Michael Bisutti, the more I adored him.

There was still one thing we needed to do, though. Mike had already met my whole family, but aside from his dad and step-mom, I had yet to get to know his other relatives. Mike's parents were divorced, and he wanted to start my "initiation" by having me spend time with his mother.

Although Mike and most of his family lived in Los Angeles, he also had a lakefront home in Montana, where he decided to host the meet and greet. With his love of the outdoors and wide-open spaces, Mike felt more at home in Montana than he did in LA. And with the stakes as high as they were that weekend, he wanted to feel as comfortable as possible.

"You're not nervous, are you?" Mike asked, holding my hand on the drive from the airport. But there was a quiver in his voice that gave away his own nerves.

"A little," I confessed. *What if his mom doesn't like me? What if she thinks I'm too young? What if she thinks this is too soon after his divorce?*

Mike interrupted my thoughts. "Don't be nervous. Mom is going to love you because I love you." He sounded confident, but I wasn't so sure.

Still, I believed that the Lord's hand had been on our relationship from the very beginning. If He could find a way to bring us together in the first place, then surely He could find a way to soften Mike's mom's heart. Besides, my grandparents were accompanying us on the trip, and it was a comfort to have them along. It was important to Mike that his mother meet not only me but my family as well. Since my parents had to work and couldn't be there themselves, Mike invited Grandma and Grandpa to come along in their place.

As it turned out, Mike's mom, Diana, was lovely in every sense of the word, and our families blended beautifully. Mike cooked a delicious pasta dinner for us, and we all laughed at the funny stories his mother shared about him as a little boy. Not to be outdone, my grandma shared a few embarrassing stories about me as well. As we lingered at the dinner table, the thought struck me: *This is family.*

At the end of the visit, we headed to the airport to say our good-byes.

"I hope to see you again soon," Diana said, giving me a hug.

After several more good-byes, Mike and I were the only ones left.

"So, am I in?" I asked as I snuggled into his arms.

"Of course." Mike grinned at me. "I told you there was nothing to worry about."

The next morning, when I emerged from the guest room in search of coffee, Mike was nowhere to be found. It was our last day together before I had to fly back to Las Vegas, so I figured he had something special planned. I looked out the kitchen window and saw Mike doing something on his pontoon boat. When he looked up, I waved.

"Good morning, beautiful!" he called. "Go get ready. We're going out for breakfast."

It was a beautiful morning in late August—hot but with very little humidity. As soon as I slid into the booth at a local restaurant, Mike slid in next to me. I couldn't help but smile— I'd always made fun of couples who sat on the same side of the booth. Now we were one of them, and I couldn't have been happier. After we finished eating, we walked around the quaint little town, shopping in some of the local boutiques and just enjoying being together.

As the afternoon sun started sinking behind the nearby mountains, I was overwhelmed at how blessed I was to have Mike in my life. I knew that God forgives and that He'd wiped my slate clean from the relationship mistakes I'd made in the past. I had experienced that firsthand years ago. But I had no idea how fully and completely He could restore and redeem—until now.

As we got a little closer to the car, my thoughts were interrupted by Mike's voice.

"Tonight I'm going to take you out for a really nice dinner, so dress up!"

Neither one of us was really the dress-up type, so this was a fairly unusual request. Since most of our dates up to this point had consisted of casual dinners out or at home with both of us in T-shirts and jeans, I figured tonight was going to be special.

I had no idea.

⁓❧⁓

I had just put on a white summer dress when Mike knocked on the door to see if I was ready.

"Yep, come on in," I called through the door.

Mike opened the door, took one look at me, and froze.

"Wow." He was smiling from ear to ear. "I have never seen anyone more beautiful in my entire life."

At dinner that night, I felt like a princess in a fairy tale. As Mike and I talked and laughed and held hands in the candlelit restaurant, I wished the night would never end.

"Why don't we head back to the house, pack some coffee ice cream, and head out on the boat so we can enjoy the sunset out on the water?" Mike suggested.

"That sounds amazing."

Once we'd cruised to a particularly scenic spot out on the lake, Mike secured the boat, pulled out a guitar he'd hidden under one of the seats, and said, "I have a surprise for you."

"You play guitar?" I asked, wondering why he'd never mentioned it before.

"Well, I do now." He started to strum the strings as he spoke. "I remembered you saying in Cancún that you had a soft spot for guys who play guitar, so I've been learning how to play."

I was speechless.

"I wrote you a song," he went on. "About us. I want to play it for you."

As he strummed his guitar, I could feel my heart keeping beat with the music. Then Mike started singing:

You with your ways . . . so loving and tender in everything
  you do.
You amaze me to no end . . . my life, my love, my friend.
I remember the first time I saw your beautiful face.
Your grace is alive and begging me to be the man I want
  to be.
Breathing life into qualities I thought inside had died.
Inspired hope and love inside this longing heart of mine.
Surely God has brought you into my life. I'm so grateful you
  are mine.

As he strummed the final chord on his guitar, he looked at me. I could see he had tears in his eyes—so did I. Just then, he put down the guitar, dropped to one knee, and pulled a ring box from his pocket. Then he opened it, revealing the most beautiful diamond ring I'd ever seen.

Is this really happening? I wondered. *Please, God, let this be real.*

"Kylie, my sweet love, will you make me the happiest man in the world and be my wife?"

"Yes!" I could barely answer through my tears as he slipped the ring onto my left hand. "I'd be honored."

We sealed the moment with a kiss as the sun continued its descent. I wanted to climb one of the mountains surrounding us and shout at the top of my lungs, "I am going to be Mrs. Michael Bisutti!"

As I leaned into my fiancé's arms and gazed up at the star-filled sky, my heart was utterly full. I silently prayed, *Father, thank You for taking my broken heart and restoring it so I could share my life with this man.*

The fairy tale was almost complete. I had found my Prince Charming. It was time for our new life to begin.

Chapter 16

MRS. KYLIE BISUTTI

God has made everything beautiful for its own
time. He has planted eternity in the human heart,
but even so, people cannot see the whole scope
of God's work from beginning to end.

ECCLESIASTES 3:11, NLT

I FELL IN LOVE with the gown the moment I saw it in the Amy
Michelson catalog. It didn't look anything like the wedding dresses
I'd modeled in Japan—all frilly and elaborate, like fashions out of
a Disney movie. No, the gown I selected was simple, understated,
and elegant—perfect for a beach wedding in sunny Cabo San
Lucas. The gown, however, was the easy part.

I'd heard plenty of warnings that it can be really stressful to
plan a wedding and that it takes most couples an entire year to
get everything ready for their big day. Mike and I knew that our
wedding, while it would be a very significant occasion, would last
for only one day. We didn't want to spend our entire engagement
obsessing over every detail and decision. Besides, it sounded more
like our style to have a casual ceremony with about forty of our

relatives and closest friends. So we landed on the obvious choice: a destination wedding.

Once we got the wedding plans nailed down, we spent most of our time planning our honeymoon. This would be the beginning of our marriage—where we'd start laying the foundation for our relationship—and we wanted to make sure those first couple of weeks were as special and romantic as possible. As March approached, our wedding was completely planned and our honeymoon was all set up. Now we just had to count down the days until we'd be husband and wife.

But things don't always turn out as planned, especially when it comes to weddings. As the date of the wedding approached, we started hearing rumblings about one of the details we had no control over.

As it turned out, Mexico was playing host not only to our May wedding, but also to one of the worst outbreaks of swine flu on record. Mike and I were still ready to tie the knot on our planned day, but some of our family members were wary of being in Mexico with all the stories of an apocalyptic health crisis flashing on the news.

When I realized we'd have to postpone our wedding, all the wedding stress I thought I'd managed to avoid came crashing down on me. Mike and I had been so excited about joining our lives together under God, and I'd been dreaming about our wedding for months now. I didn't want to wait a minute longer!

Then Mike came up with a plan.

"Well, there's only one thing to do," he said. "We'll just have a small, private ceremony at the house in Montana before the bigger one in Cabo. What do you say?"

I didn't have to think twice. "I love it!" I hugged him tightly.

If there was anything better than marrying Mike, it was marrying him twice.

And so, a couple of weeks later, with Mike's dad serving as officiant, Mike and I exchanged our vows. I officially became Mrs. Kylie Bisutti.

It might not have been Cabo on the beach, but it was every bit as special. Even more special, in fact, than I'd been imagining. After all I'd been through with Jake, I was grateful God had given me a second chance to commit myself to Him and to save myself for the man I'd spend the rest of my life with. My heart was full, thankful for God's grace.

Over the next several weeks, Mike and I continued to grow in our love for each other and in our relationship with the Lord. We made it a priority to read and study God's Word together, and we dove into various marriage books. We also found a church in Montana to attend and started getting involved there. The bright lights and hectic pace of New York City seemed a million miles away, and that was fine by me. As far as I was concerned, nothing in the world could compare to building a home and a life with the man I loved. And as if my cup weren't already overflowing, we were now only days away from our *second* wedding—this one in Cabo.

When we arrived at the beautiful Azul Resort in Cabo, I was almost as giddy as the night Mike and I first met. It was more than a year later, but I still melted like butter every time he looked at me with those beautiful dark eyes.

"By this time tomorrow, you'll officially be Mrs. Kylie Ann Bisutti . . . *again*," Mike whispered in my ear as we looked over the balcony.

"I can't wait." I rested my head against his chest.

Surprisingly, the fact that we'd already exchanged vows privately more than a month ago didn't diminish the excitement of the moment one bit. If anything, having spent the past month together as husband and wife had only intensified my emotions. Perhaps it was because I now had a deeper understanding of what this commitment meant. It wasn't just a wedding; it was a holy union—two people joined together by God.

As I reflected on the past several years, there was no doubt in my mind that Mike and I were together wholly and solely because of the Lord. There was no other possible explanation. The timing was too perfect and the paths that connected us far too intricate to be explained any other way.

Three years before, I'd thought my world was going to end. And now my life was fuller, richer, and more wonderful than I could have ever imagined. It was, in a word, miraculous.

⟡

The ceremony began at sunset in an open-air chapel overlooking the ocean. With a soft sea breeze blowing through my hair, I walked down the aisle toward the love of my life. Mike stood, handsome as ever, waiting for me with tears in his eyes and a smile on his face.

The moment was all the more special when we were joined at the altar by Mike's dad, who had graciously agreed to officiate our ceremony *again*, and by my mom, who as my best friend in the world was the obvious choice for my matron of honor.

All the fairy tales and romantic movies I'd adored my whole life paled in comparison to the moment I placed my hands in Mike's and looked into his eyes.

Mike's dad began to speak. "Dearly beloved, we are gathered together here, in the sight of God, to join together this man and this woman in holy matrimony, which is an honorable estate, instituted by God, signifying the mystical union between Christ and His church. . . ."

When I slipped the wedding band on Mike's finger, my eyes filled with tears. It was such a fitting symbol—an unbroken circle, with no beginning and no end, that said to the world, "We belong to each other. Always and forever."

After Mike's dad prayed over us and our family and friends cheered our new status as husband and wife, Mike took me in his arms and gave me a kiss that I wished could have lasted forever—and it might have, if our families hadn't broken into thunderous applause, cuing the start of the reception.

While the guests made their way to the restaurant, Mike and I stayed behind on the beach for our wedding photos. I had done hundreds of photo shoots in my life, but none of them compared to the feeling of being photographed alongside Mike as his wife.

After we were finished with the photos, we joined the rest of the party at the restaurant and enjoyed a lovely dinner with our families.

"And now I'd like to invite the bride and groom to share their first dance as husband and wife," the DJ announced.

"May I have this dance?" Mike flashed me his gorgeous smile.

"Of course," I answered.

We kicked off our shoes and walked onto the white sandy beach as the DJ played the song Mike had written and recorded for me. Then, just when I thought the evening couldn't possibly get any more magical, a magnificent fireworks display lit up the night sky.

As I watched the last of the fireworks explode overhead, I sent up a silent prayer: *Thank You, God. Thank You for blessing me with this godly man. Thank You for making this dream come true.*

Chapter 17

THE CHANCE OF A LIFETIME

Watch out for your great enemy, the devil.
He prowls around like a roaring lion,
looking for someone to devour.

1 PETER 5:8, NLT

THE MONTHS FOLLOWING our wedding were some of the happiest of my life. Even with my wedding dress wrapped up and hanging in the closet, I still felt like a princess. I had a wonderful husband I adored, and I was basking in what it meant to be truly known and loved. I felt closer to my family than I had in years, and my relationship with God was growing stronger every day. My dreams of becoming a famous runway model had all but faded into the background, and I felt content with that.

And then the enemy hit me with a greater temptation than I could have possibly imagined.

Mike and I were visiting his dad and stepmom, Susan, and while all of us were chatting in the kitchen, Susan suddenly stopped midsentence. "Oh, Kylie, I almost forgot," she said. "I have something for you." She reached for her purse, pulled out a card, and handed it to me.

I looked at the card, and my heart instantly skipped a beat. Emblazoned in bold print on the iconic pink-and-white-striped background were the two simple words that would change my life forever: "Angel Search."

"I was in Victoria's Secret the other day, and I saw a promotional poster about an upcoming Victoria's Secret Angel competition," Susan explained. "I told the girl behind the counter, 'My daughter-in-law is a model, and she looks just like an Angel.' The girl told me to have you enter the competition."

Susan shrugged her shoulders. "Anyway, I didn't know if you'd be interested or not, but I wanted to at least let you know about it."

I flipped over the card and read the details on the back:

Search Overview: Victoria's Secret is searching for a Runway Angel to appear in the Victoria's Secret Fashion Show television special! We will conduct four open casting sessions in four cities this October and accept video entries online. Our expert panel of judges will select ten promising models to participate in "Model Boot Camp" in New York City this November, where they will be videotaped/photographed as they live together, get training and modeling tips from the very best, and compete with each other to showcase their skills. The public will view footage/shots and vote to decide which finalist will be a Runway Angel in the Victoria's Secret Fashion Show television special.

All it took was one look at that entry form, and every deep-seated craving for fame, glory, and attention I thought I'd set aside for good came roaring back in full force. It wasn't enough to be a princess. I wanted to be an Angel.

"What do you think?" I asked Mike, looking at him expectantly.

"If you want to, sweetie, go for it," Mike said. "It couldn't hurt to at least try out, right?"

Looking back, I'm certain that if he'd had any idea what it would entail for me to become a Victoria's Secret Angel, he would have had a very different response. But then again, *I* would have too.

I read a little farther on the card. "It says here that the West Coast audition is in two days—in Beverly Hills."

"That's no problem," Mike said. "I have to work, but I'm sure my sister could go with you." Mike was thinking practically. My concerns were more . . . aesthetic.

"I'd have to figure out what to wear!" I pored over the info on the card again. "Two days. I'll need to go to the gym, get a spray tan . . ." And just like that, I was back in model mode. Poor Mike had no idea what had just been unleashed.

"Do you want to grab some lunch, Ky?" Mike asked.

"Sure." I glanced down at my belly and my hips. It had been quite some time since I'd really worked out, and Mike and I had been eating well. Too well. *Two days!* "I'd better just have a salad though."

I had forgotten just how slippery this slope could be.

"Do you want to see the bathing suit I bought for the audition?" I asked Mike, giving him a quick kiss as I came through the front door of our LA home.

"Sure."

I quickly changed into the blue floral bathing suit, which really popped against my newly spray-tanned skin. When I emerged from the bedroom, I got exactly the reaction I wanted.

"Wow!" Mike shook his head in mock disbelief. "You look amazing, babe. If they don't choose you, it's their loss."

"Thanks." I shot him a smile and checked my reflection in the bedroom mirror. I definitely wasn't at my thinnest, but I wasn't at my heaviest, either. Besides, I knew that Victoria's Secret models tended to be a little curvier than the typical runway model, so I wasn't overly concerned. *This is one audition where having some hips might actually work to my advantage,* I thought.

Mike's stepsister Mason was scheduled to meet me at the house and ride with me to the hotel in about an hour, so I quickly packed everything I thought I might need. *High heels—check. Hair extensions—check. Bathing suit—check. And Mason is bringing all the makeup and styling tools, so that should about do it.*

Just then Mason pulled up and honked the horn.

"Okay." Mike wrapped me in a big hug. "I'll miss you. Good luck! Call me when it's over, okay?"

"Thanks," I said. "I love you."

"I love you, too."

Minutes later, Mason and I were en route to Beverly Hills.

"Are you nervous?" Mason asked, scanning stations on the radio.

"A little," I admitted. "I've been out of the game for more than a year now, and this is unquestionably the biggest audition I've ever had. But almost all the casting agents in New York told me I walked like a Victoria's Secret model, so at least I've got that part down."

After what seemed like hours, we finally made it to the hotel. We ate a light dinner and turned in. If there was ever a night I needed my beauty sleep, this was it. As I drifted off, I prayed, *Lord, thank You for this opportunity. Whatever happens tomorrow, please let it be Your will. Amen.*

The next morning Mason gave me the full-on glam treatment—caramel-blonde hair extensions, false eyelashes, the works.

"Well, what do you think?" I asked, twisting in front of the full-length mirror. I had opted to wear a Victoria's Secret cashmere top and a black pencil skirt that would not only look flattering on me but also offer a nod to the brand for the judges.

"I think you look perfect." Mason checked her watch. "We'd better get moving. It's getting late, and who knows what the turnout is going to be like."

Mason was right. Even though we arrived in plenty of time, the line of young hopefuls was already wrapped all the way around the building.

"I bet there are more than a thousand girls here," I said, scanning the crowd. I was shocked to see that some of them were actually dressed in lingerie.

"I'll drop you off at the end of the line, and then I'll go park the car, okay?" Mason pulled up to the curb.

"Sounds good." As I gathered my things and jumped out of the car, my heart started to quicken. I took my place directly behind a tall blonde who was wearing a miniskirt that barely covered everything, along with a pair of thigh-high boots. Directly in front of her was a girl wearing a string bikini and a pair of bright-red stilettos. I had my bathing suit in my bag, but I never dreamed girls would be wearing things like that in line. A few minutes later a curvy brunette wearing fishnet stockings; leather shorts; a leather halter top; and tall, black patent leather boots stepped in line behind me.

What must the people driving by think? I wondered.

One thing was for sure: this definitely wasn't like any casting call I'd been to before. And yet one aspect of it felt all too familiar—not one of these girls was there to make friends. This was a competition in every sense of the word, complete with withering stares, sneers, and the occasional eye roll. *This is going to be a long morning,* I thought.

Surprisingly, the line moved quickly, and as I got closer to the front, I could see why. There were two casting directors positioned at the entrance of the hotel, asking the contenders to walk for them. After each potential model took a few paces, the directors pointed in one of two directions—to the right, and she'd move on to the next level; to the left, and she was out. From what I could see, there were a lot of girls headed to the left.

Stay calm, I told myself. *Lord, please help me not to be nervous.*

Finally, it was my turn.

"Okay," one of the casting directors said to me. "You're up. Show us your walk."

I took a deep breath and did my best runway walk. I knew how to walk exactly the way the Victoria's Secret Angels did—all hips, eyes, and attitude. Before I'd even finished, both directors pointed to the right. *Yes!* I was in.

When I entered the lobby, I saw a handful of other contestants milling about. I couldn't believe I'd made it to the next round.

Oh, wow. This is really it! I thought, trying not to hyperventilate.

"Here's the paperwork we need you to fill out before the next round." One of the casting directors handed me a stack of papers attached to a clipboard.

"Thanks." I smiled politely, hoping he didn't notice the tremor in my hand when I reached for the clipboard.

I need to sit down, I thought, scanning the lobby for a vacant chair. My hands were shaking so much I could hardly fill out the forms. I couldn't tell if it was nerves, excitement, or the fact that I hadn't eaten in almost fifteen hours. *I would give anything for a glass of orange juice,* I thought, looking for a beverage table. Then, out of the corner of my eye, I saw a familiar face staring at me from across the room.

"Asia!" I hopped up and ran across the lobby to hug her.

"Kylie!" she said. "I thought that was you, girl. How have you been?"

"I've been great! I got married this summer."

"Oh my gosh!" she gushed. "Congrats! I heard you were modeling in New York. Are you still there?"

"I was, but after I met Mike, I decided not to go back. How about you? Are you still in Vegas?"

"Actually, I'm living here in LA now." She looked around the room at our competition. "It looks like we made it through the first phase!"

"I know!" I beamed. "Can you believe it? We used to joke about becoming Victoria's Secret models back in Vegas, and now here we are."

"I'm telling you, girl. This was meant to be."

After about twenty minutes, one of the casting directors came in and handed each of us a Victoria's Secret robe and asked us to change into our bathing suits. As she passed out the robes, I glanced around the room to size up the competition. *There must have been well over a thousand girls in line this morning,* I thought. *And now there are only about thirty-five of us left!* My nerves had returned.

I wished I had one of my Victoria's Secret bathing suits with me, but they were all back at the lake house. *Well, at least Mike loved this one,* I consoled myself.

After we changed and slipped on our pink-and-white-striped robes, we were instructed to sit on the bleachers against the far wall. Then, one at a time, each model got a chance to walk the mock runway that was taped out on the floor while two casting directors critiqued our style and offered coaching tips.

"Wish me luck!" Asia stood to take her turn.

Her walk was just as I remembered it—all hips and Victoria's Secret material. The judges seemed pleased.

Eventually it was my turn. It wasn't easy walking in sky-high heels when my nerves were in full swing, but if there was one thing I excelled at, it was working a runway.

"She's got it," I heard one of the directors say as I passed.

"Nice job," she said to me. "Go on over there." She pointed to Asia's group on the right.

By the time the rest of the girls had walked, it was clear which of the two groups would be moving on and which would not. The competition had been winnowed down to twenty people, and Asia and I were still in the game.

"Congratulations on making it this far," the director said. "For the next phase, we'll have a mock fashion show with lights, music, and a real runway. It will take us a while to set up, so feel free to enjoy some muffins and bagels." He motioned to a table loaded with juice, water, and assorted bagels and pastries.

I was famished, but I didn't dare eat any of the snacks they'd provided, fearing it might be some kind of a test to see if we would give in and load up on carbs. Besides, I didn't want to chance looking bloated in my bathing suit, so I settled for a bottle of water.

Boy, I really could go for some of Mike's famous pasta right now, I thought.

As minutes turned to hours, the waiting became sheer torture. But Asia and I tried to make the best of it, catching up and reminiscing on old times back in Vegas. Then one of the casting directors came over and pulled me aside.

"Come with me," she said.

Uh-oh, I thought. *Please don't tell me they changed their minds.*

"Here's the deal," she whispered somewhat conspiratorially. "We want you to do really well in this competition, but we don't particularly like your bathing suit." She handed me a pink and purple Victoria's Secret bikini. "We'd like to see you in this one."

"Oh." I took the bikini from her, smiling in relief. "Thank you."

It was a perfect fit. I showed it to the casting directors, and they nodded in agreement, so I rejoined the group to get ready for the next round.

Well, that has to be a good sign, I thought. I noticed they'd done the same thing for one other girl in the group.

Before I had time to touch base with Asia again, the lights dimmed and music filled the room. It was time. I laid my robe on the bleachers and took my place in line, sporting the number seven. *Thank goodness I don't have to go first.*

One at a time, each contestant walked to the end of the runway, then stopped to answer a few questions before walking back and leaving the stage. I tried to hear the questions so I could be better prepared when my turn came, but I couldn't make out anything over the music.

Lord, help me not to be so nervous, I prayed. *And please let Your will be done, not mine.*

"Number seven," one of the casting directors called.

I took a deep breath and started out on the runway—strutting, winking, pointing into the imaginary crowd, and blowing kisses. It was the quintessential Victoria's Secret walk. When I got to the end of the runway, the two executives and the casting directors were all smiles.

"Very nice." Ed Razek, one of the bigwigs at Victoria's Secret, nodded approvingly. "You have one of the best walks I've ever seen. Do you watch our runway shows?"

"Absolutely." I hoped my voice wasn't trembling too much.

"Which model has your favorite walk?" he asked.

"Adriana Lima," I answered without hesitation. I loved Adriana's walk.

"Can you imitate her walk for us?"

"Sure." It wouldn't be hard since I'd modeled my walk after hers to begin with.

I took a deep breath and worked the runway one more time, this time amping it up even more—working the nonexistent crowd with everything I had. Then, when I reached the end of the runway, I stopped and popped the double hip like Adriana often did.

"Nice," Ed Razek said. "That was excellent."

"Thank you," I responded before heading back to the bleachers to watch for Asia's turn on the runway.

As I expected, Asia did great. I couldn't have been happier for her—for both of us, actually. I had no idea how many girls would be selected from each audition site, but the fact that the directors seemed to like both of us gave me hope that we might move on to the next stage together. It had been nice to have a friendly face to offset the usual cattiness and ferocity of the industry. And past experience had given me no reason to expect anything less at the next level of competition.

"All right, ladies," one of the casting directors called out. "That's a wrap. If you are selected to be one of the ten girls to compete for the Runway Angel title, you'll get a call from us sometime this week. Thanks so much. You were all lovely."

Ten girls, I thought, quickly doing the math. There had been twenty finalists here, and I knew there were also auditions taking place in New York City, in Chicago, in Miami, and online. With twenty finalists per location, there could be as many as a hundred finalists. My mind was whirling.

And my stomach was growling. It was already late afternoon, and I hadn't eaten a thing since my salad the night before. Just then, as I was fantasizing about an In-N-Out burger, Victoria's Secret VP Monica Mitro pulled me aside.

"That bathing suit looks really great on you," she said. "Why don't you keep it."

"Wow, thanks!" I exclaimed. "I'd love that."

I glanced over and noticed that the other girl who had been given a bikini to wear had been asked to give hers back. I wondered if that meant anything. *Is this a hint? Or a consolation prize?* I wondered. *Lord, please let it be a hint.*

The audition had gone on for so long that Mason had left the car behind and gotten a friend to pick her up. I didn't blame her. Neither of us had expected the audition to last all day. Still, I was dying to talk to someone. I grabbed my cell phone and called Mike. "Hey," I said when he picked up. "It's over."

"How'd it go?"

"Well, Ed Razek told me I had one of the best walks he'd ever seen," I said, almost giddy. "And that's huge because he's used to watching Gisele Bündchen, Tyra Banks, and Heidi Klum!"

"That's awesome, babe," Mike said. I knew those names didn't mean anything to him, so I appreciated his genuine enthusiasm on my behalf. "So, when will you find out if you made the cut?"

"They said they'd call sometime in the next week," I answered. "Hopefully it won't be too long."

"I miss you," he said. "And, babe, I'm proud of you."

As I hung up, I thanked God for blessing me with such a supportive husband. He didn't fully understand what all this was about, but he knew it was important to me. And for now, anyway, that was enough.

Several days passed, and I still hadn't heard from anyone at Victoria's Secret. The tension was starting to get to me.

Mike had gone on a hunting trip, and he wanted me to come along. But since I was afraid I wouldn't get cell reception out in the woods, I stayed behind, and my mom came for a visit. By day five, I couldn't take it anymore. I had to get out of the house—even if only for a few minutes—so my mom suggested we swing through the Starbucks drive-through for some fresh air and a quick caffeine boost.

Just as I finished placing our order, my phone started vibrating. It was a number I didn't recognize.

"Hello," I answered, juggling my phone in one hand and handing my money out the window with the other.

"Is this Kylie Bisutti?" a woman asked.

"Yes, it is." I handed Mom our drinks.

"I'm calling on behalf of the Victoria's Secret Runway Angel competition. Congratulations—you made it! You will be one of the ten girls living in the Victoria's Secret Angel house in New York City, competing for the title."

There was a momentary pause while I tried to wrap my head around what she'd just said.

"Kylie?" she said. "Are you excited?"

"Yes!" I tried not to scream into the phone. "Oh, I can't believe it! Thank you so much!"

"We'll be flying you to New York in a few days," she continued. "In the meantime, you'll need to get a physical and have some basic blood work done. I'll e-mail you the rest of the information. Congrats again, Kylie. We'll see you soon."

"Thanks for the call," I said, still slightly in shock.

I turned to Mom. She had tears in her eyes.

"I'm in!" I screamed. "I'm one of the ten girls they chose to compete in New York!"

Mom reached across the car and hugged me.

"I am so happy for you, Ky." Her eyes were gleaming.

"I have to call Mike!" My hands were shaking so much I hardly could push the buttons on my phone. "Oh, please let him have cell phone reception."

The phone rang twice, and then Mike picked up.

"Mike, I made it!" I squealed.

"That's great!" he responded. "So what does this mean? What happens next?"

"They're flying me to New York," I said. "I have to be there in two days."

"That soon, huh?" He paused. "That means I won't be home before you leave. I won't be able to say good-bye to you in person."

I hadn't thought about that. "I'm so sorry, honey."

"Do you know how long you'll be gone?"

"I'm not sure—a couple of weeks at least."

"Well, do what you need to do, sweetie." Mike tried to sound as upbeat and encouraging as possible, but I knew he was thinking the same thing I was: this would be the longest we'd be apart since we got married. "I'm going to miss you so much. I hope you know how much I love you."

"I love you, too." I was going to miss him like crazy. *Thank You, God, for bringing me Mike.*

The next two days were a blur. With my physical exam and blood work out of the way, I frantically started packing for New York. I had no idea what to bring, and the e-mail I'd received contained very few details about what we'd be doing or how we should dress. *Might as well play it safe,* I figured. So I took a little of everything—high heels, tennis shoes, jeans, dresses, bathing suits, a heavy coat, workout clothes, and pretty much everything I owned that came from Victoria's Secret.

There, I thought, surveying the wreckage of my room. *I think that's everything.* Correction—almost everything. I grabbed my Bible. If ever there was a time I would need God at my side, this was definitely it.

Chapter 18

THE FIRST CHALLENGE

Now we see things imperfectly, like puzzling
reflections in a mirror, but then we will see
everything with perfect clarity. All that I know
now is partial and incomplete, but then I will
know everything completely, just as
God now knows me completely.

I CORINTHIANS 13:12, NLT

LESS THAN FORTY-EIGHT HOURS after receiving the news that I'd
made the top ten, I found myself on the red-eye bound for New
York City. Staring out the window into the darkness, I pondered
my last trip to the Big Apple. It seemed like eons ago, and after
I met Mike, I honestly didn't think I'd ever go back.

I glanced at my wedding ring, a tangible symbol of the most
significant change in my life over the past eighteen months.
I closed my eyes and silently prayed, *Lord, thank You for all the
blessings You've given me. Thank You for Mike, for my family, and for
this incredible opportunity. Please help me to do what's right and to
keep seeking Your plan for my life. I don't know what the future holds,
but I do know that You hold the future. Please guide my footsteps, and
let Your will be done through me. Amen.*

When I landed in New York, I picked up my luggage, headed to the area I'd been told about in the e-mail, and got my first look at the rest of the group. I was disappointed to see that Asia wasn't there. *Too bad,* I thought. *It would have been so nice to have a friend to go through this with me.*

Within minutes a van arrived to pick us up and take us to downtown Manhattan. For a brief moment our excitement over-ruled our competitive instincts, and we introduced ourselves to one another. As it turned out, I wasn't the only newlywed. One of the other girls, Tika, had also gotten married recently.

"I already miss my husband," Tika said, moving to a seat next to me.

"Me, too," I agreed. "We had to leave so quickly, I wasn't even able to say good-bye." I looked at my wedding ring, sparkling in the morning sunlight. It was true—I missed Mike already.

Hearing the sounds of the city and seeing all the familiar places made me feel slightly nostalgic. *I wonder if Brittany is still model-ing,* I mused. I thought about my homeless friends and hoped they were okay. I also wondered if word had gotten back to Red Model that I was one of the top-ten finalists in the Angel competition.

My reverie was cut short when the van stopped in front of the hotel where we would be spending the evening. Then our first order of business was announced: psych evaluations.

With more than three hundred questions, the written portion of the evaluation was overwhelming. "How is your life at home?" "Do you now or have you ever suffered from any form of depres-sion?" "How often do you experience anxiety?" "Do you ever suf-fer from panic attacks?" *Wow,* I thought. *They're really concerned about our mental stability. What, exactly, is going to happen in this competition?*

Growing up,
I was all legs
and skinny as a
beanpole.

One of my first official glamour shots at age thirteen

Back in my Fashion
Mall modeling days.
That's me in the cowboy
hat and tank top, and
Asia is standing next to
me in the red jacket.

Here I am after a
photo shoot in Japan
at age sixteen.

In Huntington Beach
with my small group
leader, Teresa, the day I
was baptized

Goofing around in the subway on my first day as a model in New York City

My little brother, Luke, giving me a kiss over Christmas vacation in 2010. I can't believe I let my obsession with my weight and my career take priority over this little sweetie.

Mike and me with my parents at our wedding in Cabo

Getting a kiss from Luke after the wedding

With my cousin Monique, whose comment about wanting to stop eating so she could look like me made me realize what a terrible role model I was being

The greatest day of my life

The ten finalists in the Victoria's Secret Runway Angel competition. Top row (l-r): me, Krystina Holbrook, Catharina Lee, Alicia Hall, Raven Ervin, Courtney O'Connor. Front row (l-r): Allison Turner, Katelyn Fortes, Jamie Lee Darley, Tika Ivezaj.

Working out with David Kirsch. This was by far my favorite challenge!

Behind the scenes of the Victoria's Secret Fashion Show – following my eight-hour makeover

Wearing my leather Victoria's
Secret Angel jacket

At the premier of *Serious Moonlight*
in 2009 looking freakishly thin

Sharing my heart with
George Stephanopolous
on *Good Morning America*

Today—happy, healthy, and His

After finishing my survey and meeting briefly with a psychologist, who essentially asked me the same questions the written evaluation contained, I was emotionally drained and in dire need of fresh air. I decided to change into my workout clothes and hit the hotel gym. When my physical exhaustion matched my mental exhaustion, I returned to my room and gave Mike a quick call to let him know how much I missed him. Then I spent a few minutes reading my Bible and collapsed into bed.

The next morning we were instructed to pack our belongings and meet in the lobby. Once we all were present, we piled into a black van that would take us to our new home for the next six weeks. As soon as the van doors slid open, the cameras started rolling. Our private lives were officially over, and our public lives had begun.

If the film crew was hoping for a big reaction from us when we saw the Victoria's Secret apartment for the first time, they weren't disappointed. Located in the heart of the Financial District, it was the largest apartment I'd ever seen. The place covered two stories, with two huge bedrooms, a spacious living room, a state-of-the-art kitchen, and three large bathrooms—all fully stocked with a wide assortment of Victoria's Secret lotions, creams, washes, fragrances, and shampoos. The living room alone was larger than the entire apartment I'd shared with Brittany, and it was almost triple the size of the tiny hovel VMM had set me up in three years ago. *Things definitely get better at the top,* I thought.

Everything inside was absolutely pristine—white marble tiles, white walls and cabinets, and white furniture, all accented with pink pillows, vases, and other assorted knickknacks. Along the walls were enormous framed pictures of the most famous Angels—a constant reminder of why we were there.

"This is gorgeous!" Tika exclaimed.

"I love it!" I echoed.

We quickly splintered off into two groups and headed to the bedrooms to choose our beds and unpack. Waiting for each of us was a plush Victoria's Secret robe and a small pink-and-white-striped gift bag with our name on it. Mine contained a matching leopard-print bra and panty set. I had a hunch that this wasn't just a housewarming gift—that it might have something to do with an upcoming photo shoot.

We were also informed of a few specific house rules we were expected to abide by:

1. No visitors were allowed.
2. There were to be no cameras of any kind.
3. We were forbidden to tell anyone except our immediate families where we were staying. Our families were allowed to have only our mailing address.
4. Curfew was at 10 p.m.—no exceptions.

We were given a few moments to unpack and settle in before a member of the Victoria's Secret "Glam Crew" came in to tell us about our first challenge.

"Hi, ladies," she announced, clapping her hands to get our attention and bring us into full view of the cameras. "Welcome to your new home. Your first task starts tonight. Get your things and follow me."

As instructed, we ran back to our rooms to change into the lingerie we'd been given, along with a Victoria's Secret sweat suit. Each of us had been given a different color sweat suit—mine was a pretty pink. After slipping into my leopard-print set, I gave myself a once-over in the bathroom mirror. The bombshell bra they'd given me increased my normal C cup by two full sizes. Feeling a little self-conscious, I zipped up my sweat suit, grabbed my robe, and headed for the door.

It was close to 11 p.m. by the time we loaded onto a bus bound for the undisclosed location of our first challenge. When the bus stopped, I looked out the window and, to my surprise, discovered we were at Grand Central Station. That's when it hit me. *Wait a minute. We're going to model lingerie in the middle of Grand Central Station?* My mind flashed to my exaggerated cup size, and I froze, my arms instinctively crossing over my chest.

I would have given anything for a few moments alone to collect my thoughts, but the cameras were rolling, and as was the case in every location shoot, time was money.

The handlers ushered us off the bus, much to the delight of the raucous late-night crowd milling about the Station's main terminal. The lighting equipment had already been set up, awaiting our arrival. Whatever reservations I had were put on hold instantly as I looked into the television camera that tracked my every move. In a competition determined solely by public opinion and popular votes, it wouldn't help my cause to look anything other than happy, confident, and angelic. *It's just nerves,* I thought, trying to reassure myself. *Once the camera is turned on you, you'll be fine.*

Still, I couldn't stop trembling. And it wasn't just because it was late October in New York.

After shuffling us all into position, Ed Razek appeared and introduced us to Doutzen Kroes, our Angel hostess for the evening. I was in awe. She was even more beautiful in person than she was in the catalogs. Now the pressure was really starting to mount.

Seriously? My first ever Victoria's Secret shoot, and both Ed Razek and Doutzen Kroes will be watching? But that wasn't all.

"You're going to be photographed tonight by world-renowned fashion photographer Russell James," Ed continued. As Russell James walked over to stand next to Ed and Doutzen, my head began to spin. Talk about pressure. Suddenly the psych evaluation was making a lot more sense.

While Russell made last-minute adjustments to the lighting equipment, Doutzen offered us a few tips on how to play to the lights and to pose in a way that would best showcase the lingerie. I'd always loved the technical aspect of modeling, so I hung on her every word.

Each of us had only five minutes to pose for the camera and—hopefully—for Russell to get the perfect shot. While I was on deck, waiting for my turn in front of the camera, Doutzen motioned for me. I did a double take.

Me? I mouthed, pointing to myself. *Yes, you,* she mouthed back, waving me over.

"Hi, Kylie, I'm Doutzen," she said.

"Hi," I responded shyly. "It's nice to meet you."

I was, admittedly, a little starstruck. Originally hailing from the Netherlands, Doutzen had been with Victoria's Secret since 2004, and I'd followed her career over the years. And now here she was, talking to *me*.

"Ed tells me you have an amazing walk," she continued. "Would you mind showing me?"

"Sure." I was a little taken aback—both by the compliment and by the request. I took a few steps back and then did my best Angel walk while Doutzen, Ed, and about a hundred onlookers watched. It was a little embarrassing, but also strangely exhilarating.

"Wow," Doutzen said. "Your walk *is* really good!"

Just then, Russell called for me. I was up.

"Good luck," Doutzen called.

As I peeled off my robe, I thought, *I have a feeling I'm going to need it.*

Knowing I had only five minutes to work with Russell, I tried to make the most of it and do everything Doutzen had coached us to do. But my nerves were getting the better of me, and my face and body kept tensing up.

"Turn your body into the light if you can," Russell coached. "More . . . more . . . just a little more. Try to soften it up a bit. Relax. Okay, good."

And just like that, my time was up. *I hope he got some decent shots,* I thought. As nervous as I'd been heading into the challenge, I wasn't ready to go home yet.

After I got back into my sweats, the camera crew called me over to say a few words to the viewers. I wasn't sure what to say, but I figured honesty was the best policy. I told them how much I'd enjoyed meeting Doutzen and getting to work with Russell, and that I hoped my shots would be good enough to keep me in the competition a little longer.

Wow, I thought, walking away from the camera. *That's going to take some getting used to.* And as I was about to learn, so would the televised critiques.

Later that week all the girls gathered in the living room to watch the photographer's comments and see which shots he chose. Meanwhile, the television crew was filming our every reaction. It was extremely uncomfortable, especially when the critiques were less than flattering.

When the photographer was asked about me, he said, "From a

physical standpoint, she has this little tiny waist and a very pretty face, though she is extremely busty. I don't know if that will play out to be a good thing or a bad thing. I also found Kylie to be a little difficult to shoot in terms of giving me that one look. But she did take direction well, and it slowly broke open."

Of course I looked busty, I thought. *That bra they gave me doubled my chest size.* When they showed the final picture he'd chosen, I was mortified. It didn't even look like me. Unbeknownst to me, they had Photoshopped my waist to look even smaller than it already was, and they had made my chest even bigger. My body didn't even look real. I knew that Photoshop was used to get rid of blemishes or scars for print ads—especially on close-ups—but I had no idea they would completely alter the way a model's body looked. Even when I'd dropped all the way down to 108 pounds, my waist hadn't been that tiny.

Nothing about that shot is real, I thought. And in a few days it was going to be broadcast all over the country. Still, with the cameras rolling, the best I could do was put on a brave face, accept the criticism, and try my best to ignore the unnatural photo of me that filled the sixty-inch flat-screen TV.

What will people think? I wondered. *What will Mike think?*

When the episode aired, Mike started getting crude text messages and e-mails from his buddies. There was no way around it—this competition was starting to heat up for both of us. While I was doing my best to grin and bear it in New York, Mike was back home, taking it to God in prayer.

Chapter 19

FRIENDS AND RIVALS

Always be prepared to give an answer to everyone who asks
you to give the reason for the hope that you have. But do
this with gentleness and respect, keeping a clear conscience,
so that those who speak maliciously against your good
behavior in Christ may be ashamed of their slander.

I PETER 3:15-16

I WASN'T THE ONLY ONE in the apartment who struggled with the
rude comments and harsh critiques. One of the younger girls,
Katelyn, seemed to be taking the criticism particularly hard. And
understandably so. It's one thing to be told you're too big or too
curvy in private, but it's another to hear those comments aired on
national television. And with the competition in full swing, there
wasn't a lot of sympathy among the other contestants.

When I saw what Katelyn was going through, I felt like I could
relate. I knew what it was like to be the youngest model in the
room—and I knew what it was like to be called fat in front of a
crowd of people. So the day after we watched Russell's critiques,
when the cameras were off, I pulled her aside and gave her a hug.

"I know you're having a really hard time right now," I said,

173

"but you've got to hang in there. This is a crazy business, and it can be incredibly cruel at times. Believe me, I've been there. My own agent once called me a cow in front of the entire office. But you know what has kept me sane through it all?"

"What?" She looked at me, wiping the tears from her cheeks.

"My relationship with God," I answered. "It's an amazing thing to be able to see yourself through God's eyes. Because God doesn't see you the way the world does—in inches and pounds. He sees in you all the things that really matter, like kindness and compassion and love. You're a beautiful girl, Katelyn, but you're also a beautiful person. And no matter how this competition ends, that's never going to change." I reached in my bag and pulled out my old copy of *Battlefield of the Mind* by Joyce Meyer.

"Here." I handed her the book. "I want you to have this. It'll help you start seeing yourself the way God does. It's all about changing the way you think."

"Thanks," she said, opening the book and leafing through it.

Truth be told, I didn't know what had possessed me to bring along that dog-eared copy of *Battlefield of the Mind* in the first place. I hadn't looked at it in ages. I still found Joyce's mind-over-matter message uplifting, but since I'd been going deeper in my faith, I had been going straight to the Word for wisdom and guidance. Even so, I hoped this book would be an accessible starting point for Katelyn in the midst of the chaos.

As I walked away from Katelyn, I noticed several of the girls all huddled in a group, looking my way and giggling. Apparently they had overheard our conversation, and judging by their reactions, I was pretty sure they'd just labeled me a Jesus freak. But I didn't care. God had changed my life forever, and I wasn't ashamed to admit it.

That same week a local news station did a feature story about the Angel competition, and it sent out a reporter and a film crew to tour the apartment and interview us. I was getting better at being "on" all the time with the cameras around, but it was wearying. Both the media and the Victoria's Secret crew constantly tried to bait us into tearing one another down, but I was determined to take the high road. Whenever I was interviewed, I tried to focus on the role my faith in God played in my life and on how much I missed my husband. And even though everyone at Victoria's Secret encouraged me not to, lest it tarnish the Angel fantasy, I proudly wore my wedding ring throughout the entire competition. I wanted to win, but not at any cost.

When the pressure really started to build, I called Mike, my mom, or my dad. They kept me grounded and gave me an outlet to express some of the frustrations I couldn't share on film. Just hearing them say "I love you" gave me the boost I needed to keep going.

I definitely wanted to win—not just for me, but for them.

Several days after our first challenge, the handlers delivered another batch of lingerie to the apartment.

"Thanks," I said, checking out the red bra and matching panties they'd chosen for me. *Another lingerie shoot?* I thought. *I wonder where this one's going to take place.*

We were instructed to put on the lingerie and head up to the roof, where a temporary runway had been set up. *On the roof? In November?* Surely it would be freezing up there. *Seriously, what do these people have against the indoors?* I wondered.

As a way to up the ante, this time we had to do our own hair and makeup—something that never has been my forte. We all squeezed into the bathrooms and took turns inadvertently blinding one another with hair spray and bumping into one another with flat irons.

After we had sufficiently glammed up, we were taken to the roof. They asked each of us to do our runway walk, snapping pictures and taking video footage as we went. It was so cold, I could see my breath. *When does the challenge start?* I wondered, frantically rubbing my hands together in a futile attempt to stay warm.

"By the way," one of the handlers announced about fifteen minutes in, "this isn't an official challenge. But it is important, so give it your best."

After I finished my turn, one of the other girls, Jamie Lee, a sweet, pretty blonde from California, was smiling at me.

"You did great," she said under her breath so the others wouldn't hear.

"Thanks," I responded. "So did you."

Huh, I thought. *At least some of the girls are genuinely nice.*

I knew that in a few days the first elimination would take place, and five girls would be sent home. With any luck, Tika, Jamie Lee, Katelyn, and I would not be among them. We still had a long way to go, and the journey would be a whole lot easier if I had a few friends.

It had been more than a week since our Grand Central Station shoot, and we were all on edge, wondering when half of us would be gone. To keep our minds occupied, Jamie Lee and I went to yoga classes, and Tika and I tried our hands at some cooking in the apartment's top-notch kitchen. Finally one of the handlers arrived with the announcement we'd all been waiting for.

"Okay, girls, your first elimination and your next challenge are officially beginning now. Please bring a bathing suit and meet me out front at the bus in ten minutes."

Bathing suits. That's a nice switch, I thought.

We grabbed our suits and coats and piled onto the bus, film crew in tow. Once again, we had no idea where we were going. *Please don't tell me they're going to have us all splashing around in the icy Hudson River.* I was relieved when the bus stopped in front of a gym on Chelsea Piers. When we walked into the building, we were greeted by Ed Razek, who immediately split us into two groups of five. I was in a group with Jamie Lee, Tika, a girl from Las Vegas named Alicia, and a girl from Missouri named Allison. Since all of us were instructed to bring our swimsuits, presumably for the next challenge, it was impossible to tell which group was staying and which was going. You could have cut the tension with a knife.

Then, out of nowhere, in walked Australian Angel extraordinaire Miranda Kerr. As if on cue, all the contestants turned toward her and started applauding.

"Congratulations," she said with a smile. "I'm so happy to see you all. You've done a wonderful job so far. As you know, the public has been voting online for their five favorite models. Those girls are about to come one step closer to the runway. But . . ." She paused. "I'm sorry to say, for the other five of you, the competition ends right here."

I took deep breaths, trying to brace myself for the news either way.

"You've been split into two groups," Miranda continued. "Five of you are staying, and five of you are going. The five of you who will be staying are Alicia, Kylie, Jamie Lee, Allison, and Tika.

Unfortunately, for the rest of you, it's time to collect your bags. I'm sorry, but you're going home."

I breathed a sigh of relief. While our group celebrated, the girls in the other group broke down in tears. Every moment was captured on film. I felt awful for the girls who didn't make it—especially Katelyn. I had hoped to have more time to talk with her.

As soon as we said our good-byes, the handlers presented each of us with some Victoria's Secret VSX workout clothes, and we were all escorted to the gym for our next challenge. Now this was a challenge I could get excited about. I enjoyed working out, and I knew my way around a gym. Nothing, however, could have prepared me for the killer workout we were about to do.

Upon our arrival, the cameras started rolling, and Miranda greeted us again.

"Hi, girls. Congratulations on making it this far, and welcome to your second challenge. It takes a lot of work to be a Victoria's Secret Runway Angel. You have to be toned, fit, and super healthy." She gave a dramatic pause. "So we've brought in a supertrainer to get you runway ready. Please welcome . . . David Kirsch!"

David Kirsch! My stomach flipped. *He's the one who got Heidi Klum runway ready after she had each of her children. I can't believe we're going to be training with him!*

"Hello, ladies. Glad to be here," David said. "I'm here to be a keen eye. I want to see what you've got and what you don't have. When you walk down that runway in your lingerie, millions of eyes are going to be watching you, and I don't want anything moving that shouldn't be moving. That includes thighs, butts, arms, and bellies. So get ready to get Kirsched!"

It turned out that the first step in getting Kirsched was stripping down to our bathing suits and letting David point out all our strengths and all our flaws—on camera.

When it was my turn, I took off my workout clothes and stood there in my red bathing suit, waiting for assessment. But before he told me what he thought, he asked me what areas I thought needed work.

"Well, my abs could probably be tighter." I scanned my midsection. "And I could be firmer overall."

"I agree that your abs could stand some tightening up," he agreed. "But on the whole, it's not that bad. Your biggest problem is your butt. It's okay—there's just not enough of it."

Unbelievable, I thought. *For the first time in my life, I'm not curvy enough!*

"As for the rest of your body," he continued. "I would agree that your back, thighs, butt, and arms could all use a fine-tune overhaul to get you runway ready. What do you say—are you ready?"

"Yep, I'm ready," I responded. At least I thought I was.

What followed was one of the most grueling workouts I'd ever attempted. We started with legs, doing lunges, squats, frog jumps, inner-thigh work, and outer-thigh work. Then we turned to the abs, shoulders, and backs, doing planks, side sit-ups, knee lifts, and push-ups. After that David had us shadowbox with hand weights for cardio. And then we did it all again. Twice.

It was the most intense workout of my life, and even though my thighs were shaking, I kept pushing. Some of the girls were laughing and making jokes out of everything, but I was in it to win it. I had been given the opportunity to work out with one of the most respected trainers in the industry, and I intended to take full advantage of it. My persistence paid off. Not only did David give me a glowing review, but I won the challenge.

"Kylie really surprised me," David said in the follow-up interview. "When I first met her, I thought, *She's beautiful, but she's a bit of a lightweight.* I definitely didn't think she was going to be able to withstand my workout, yet more than any girl here, she gave me 500 percent every single time. Kylie showed me that she has the passion to make it to that runway."

I was thrilled. This was one challenge I couldn't wait for Mike to see on TV.

David's review of some of the other models wasn't nearly as flattering. He called out a number of the girls for being overly cocky and for not taking the workout seriously. Being a Victoria's Secret Angel was about more than just having a pretty face, and several of the contestants were learning that the hard way. Now it was time to see what the audience at home thought.

The rest of the week was pretty low key. We had a considerable amount of downtime built into our schedules, which we divided evenly between working out at the gym, going to Starbucks, and lounging around the apartment waiting for the next elimination. Then one day, one of the girls decided it would be fun to visit a psychic and learn her fate ahead of time.

I was relaxing on the beanbag chair in the living room, reading my Bible, when Tika returned. She immediately came over and plopped down next to me with a disappointed look in her eyes. I could tell something was up.

"I think I did something bad today," she said sheepishly, telling me about her visit to the psychic. Tika had been raised Catholic, and getting the reading done had really upset her.

I agreed that it wasn't the best idea, but I encouraged her not to beat herself up over it. "If you ask God for forgiveness, He'll forgive you," I told her.

Then I shared my testimony with Tika. I told her how God had forgiven me—how He'd given me hope when I felt hopeless, love when I felt rejected, and peace when I felt overcome with anxiety. She listened intently, and then we quietly prayed together.

After we finished praying, Tika looked at me and said something I'll never forget. "I feel like you're going to win this whole thing, Kylie. You really are a true angel. I think God let me get this far in the competition so I could meet you and have this conversation tonight. Thank you."

My eyes filled with tears. Even if I went home after the next challenge, just hearing Tika say those words made the whole experience worth it.

Chapter 20

EARNING MY WINGS

Everyone who competes in the games goes into strict
training. They do it to get a crown that will not last,
but we do it to get a crown that will last forever.

1 CORINTHIANS 9:25

TIMES SQUARE IS OFTEN referred to as the Crossroads of the World—
and for good reason. Located in the heart of Manhattan and the
legendary Broadway theater district, it is the epicenter of the enter-
tainment industry, an advertising hub, and the most popular tourist
attraction in the world. All of which made it the perfect backdrop
for the next elimination in a competition that would catapult one
lucky contestant to instant fame as an elite representative of one of
the most iconic brands in the entire fashion world.

Standing at the corner of Broadway and Seventh Avenue,
bathed in the glow of the enormous illuminated billboards that
frame the Square, and surrounded by thousands of tourists repre-
senting countries from all over the world, we felt our hearts skip
a collective beat.

As I looked around, trying to take it all in, I noticed several Victoria's Secret personalities lingering at the edge of the crowd. One of them was veteran Angel Marisa Miller, who looked absolutely stunning. With perfect sun-kissed skin and long blonde hair, she looked every inch the California surfer girl she was. Almost as soon as we made eye contact with her, she walked over.

"Hi, girls," she said cheerily, rubbing her hands together for warmth. "Welcome to Times Square. I have the results of the second round of the online voting. Unfortunately, only two of you can remain in the competition. For the other three of you . . . I'm sorry, but the road to the runway ends right now."

We all held our breath as Marisa paused for what seemed like an eternity. "Behind me, you'll see our Victoria's Secret screens." She gestured to a series of gigantic billboards and scrolling marquees that read "Victoria's Secret Fashion Show" in glowing block letters. "The two girls who have made it through are about to have their big-screen debut. The two finalists are . . ."

We all stood with our eyes glued to the enormous screen directly behind Marisa. Suddenly the screen faded to black, and when the lights came back on, a split screen appeared, featuring side-by-side images that had been pulled from the rooftop shoot our first week.

One was Jamie Lee. The other was me.

I stared at the screen in disbelief. I had been bracing myself for the worst so I'd be able to face the cameras with dignified composure when I was eliminated. But I was completely unprepared for this.

"Congratulations, Kylie and Jamie Lee!" Marisa beamed as the video footage of the two of us strutting on the rooftop rolled behind her.

I felt a hand on my shoulder and turned to see Jamie Lee smiling at me, her eyes welling with tears. We gave each other a celebratory hug as Alicia, Allison, and Tika were escorted off to the side for their final on-air interviews. I felt bad for the other girls—Tika in particular. Watching a lifelong dream slip away was difficult enough. Having to do it in the middle of Times Square with television cameras rolling and throngs of people looking on had to be a nightmare.

I wanted to say something to Tika. She had, after all, been my closest friend throughout the competition, and at the very least I wanted to say good-bye. But before I could make my way over to her, one of the handlers herded Jamie Lee and me to a nearby trailer to prepare for our next challenge. We had already shown that we could photograph well and that we had the physical stamina to maintain the Angel physique. Now it was time to see how well we would deal with the media.

After having our makeup and hair touched up, Jamie Lee and I were each presented with an official Victoria's Secret Angel jacket. I had to admit the jacket was pretty amazing—black leather with diamond-studded wings on the back and the words *Victoria's Secret Angel* emblazoned underneath in silver embroidery. The perfect blend of toughness and femininity.

When we stepped back out of the trailer, we were greeted by a veritable choir of Angels who had come to congratulate us on making the final cut. Marisa, Doutzen, and Miranda were all there, along with Alessandra Ambrosio, Chanel Iman, Behati Prinsloo, Candice Swanepoel, and the biggest Angel of all, Heidi Klum. They were wearing the same black leather jackets we'd just been given. *Unbelievable,* I marveled. *I'm actually one of them.* Well, almost. There were still two more challenges to go, and the first one was about to begin. It was time to face the media.

Before the challenge commenced, Jamie Lee and I were ushered into Marisa's trailer for some last-minute coaching. It wasn't a coincidence that all the Angels happened to descend on Times Square at the same time. They were in town for the annual Victoria's Secret Fashion Show that was scheduled to be taped that weekend, and we would be attending the press junket right alongside them.

These models were seasoned pros. We, on the other hand, were not. And how we handled ourselves in front of the media would be a key factor in whether we would keep those diamond-studded wings.

While I felt perfectly at ease on the runway, I was extremely shy by nature and tended to clam up when asked to talk about myself or speak up in a group, so I was all ears as Marisa doled out her advice.

"Okay, ladies," she said. "As we speak, the world media is outside setting up for a photo op and press conference with the Fashion Show models and with you. Here's what you need to know. The press is trying to catch you, to get you to say things you don't want to say." She fixed her eyes intently on us. "So you have to be cautious. But you also have to be careful not to look like you're on guard. Just be yourself and let your personality shine. You guys have earned this. Now you've got to adopt the mentality that you deserve to be here. Take a breath. Relax. And just focus on being your beautiful selves."

Then, with a wink, she added one final piece of advice: "And, girls, remember to work that camera."

So . . . be fun, flirty, imperceptibly guarded, articulate, witty, and sensual. I laughed to myself. *No problem—that should be easy enough. Oh, God, please help me not to make a complete fool of myself.*

We exited the trailer into a sea of blinding camera flashes, and immediately the gauntlet was thrown down. Questions came from every direction, so fast and frenzied I could barely keep pace: "How often do you eat?" "Have you broken many hearts?" "Being a Victoria's Secret model is a huge honor, but the money won't hurt either, right?" "Who is the best-looking guy you've ever dated?" "What kind of advice would you give to an aspiring model?"

I did my best to answer honestly and simply, being careful not to say anything that could be taken out of context. I played to the crowd and to the cameras as best as I could, but I made a point of brushing my hair out of my eyes with my left hand as often as possible, hoping the sight of my wedding ring would put a damper on the relationship questions they kept firing at me.

Marisa had been right: they were searching for any kind of dirt they could get. I wasn't perfect by any means, but I could rest in the confidence that God had mercifully wiped my slate clean.

After the press conference, Jamie Lee and I were escorted to the Victoria's Secret headquarters to be fitted for the Fashion Show that weekend. While we were in the fitting room, I caught my first glimpse of the Angel wings hanging on the rack, waiting to be taken to the venue for the taping. They were even more elaborate than I'd imagined—not to mention enormous! *How do the models keep from knocking each other over when they pass on the runway?* I wondered, adding yet another item to the list of potential mishaps formulating in my mind.

Fortunately, neither Jamie Lee nor I would be sporting wings that weekend. Instead, we were both fitted with identical black-and-silver bra and panty sets, sheer-black-lace jackets, and red stilettos. If we wanted the wings, we'd have to earn them.

"You both look great," Monica Mitro commented as Jamie Lee

and I gave ourselves once-overs in the mirror. "It's going to be a great show."

I tried to catch her enthusiasm, but there was something nagging at me. And when I tried to pray, the words got stuck before they reached my throat.

Seeing the actual runway for the first time was overwhelming—a tangible reminder that in a matter of hours, we would be walking in front of a worldwide television audience numbering in the tens of millions. But of the millions of eyes that would be watching me walk down that runway, the only ones I was concerned with belonged to Mike.

Mike had never seen me walk in a runway show, and his opinion meant more to me than everyone at Victoria's Secret and in the viewing audience combined. I was thrilled beyond words that he was flying out for the show, but I was also a nervous wreck. I hadn't seen Mike for weeks, and I desperately wanted him to be proud of me.

That night at the hotel, Mike put all my fears to rest.

"You're going to do great, baby." He kissed me on the forehead. "You kicked butt in the fitness competition, and tomorrow night you're going to rock that runway." He held my face in his hands, looked deep into my eyes, and said, "Win or lose, sweetie, you'll always be an angel in my book."

Thank You, God, for Mike. He always knew exactly the right thing to say. It felt so good to have his support. And yet he knew so little about the modeling industry. I wondered if he had any idea what it would actually mean for us if I won this competition.

"You know, Mike, if I do win, things are going to get really crazy for a while," I cautioned. "Red-carpet events, autograph signings, movie premieres, photo shoots in New York, London, Paris, and all over the world. How would you feel about that?"

Mike paused for a second and then took a deep breath. "Well, I think we may need to look into getting an apartment in New York, since you'll probably be spending quite a bit of time here when you win."

"You mean *if* I win," I corrected.

"No, I mean *when* you win." He held me close.

As I lay there in Mike's arms, I felt at peace with whatever might happen. Win or lose, I knew that Mike would always love me. And ultimately, all of this was in God's hands. I was going to do my best and let Him determine the outcome.

Before I drifted off to sleep, I whispered the prayer I'd been saying for weeks. "Lord, if You want me to win this competition, then let Your will be done. Thank You for Your continued blessings. I love You. Amen."

Chapter 21

THE FINAL CHALLENGE

Trust in the LORD with all your heart
     and lean not on your own understanding;
in all your ways submit to him,
     and he will make your paths straight.

PROVERBS 3:5-6

AS MUCH AS I WOULD HAVE loved to spend the day with Mike
and show him around New York, I had a 9 a.m. makeup call
at the Lexington Avenue Armory—the venue for our final challenge. Jamie Lee and I would be walking the runway at the 2009
Victoria's Secret Fashion Show alongside the most celebrated fashion models in the world.

As I made my way to the Armory on foot, I couldn't help but
wonder, *What's with the 9 a.m. makeup call? The taping doesn't start
until 6 p.m. What could we possibly be doing for eight hours?*

I got my answer as soon as I arrived backstage. There, waiting for
us, were several twelve-foot-long tables filled with hair extensions
of every length and color imaginable. Another twelve-foot table
was filled with makeup of all kinds—blush, powder, concealer,

mascara, eyeliner, lip liner, lipstick, lip gloss, eye shadow, bronzer, false eyelashes—along with hundreds of different-sized brushes, puffs, and applicators. There also was an entire room set aside for manicures and pedicures, as well as a bronzing station, complete with a full airbrushing system.

In the midst of it all, dozens of stylists, assistants, interns, and stagehands were scurrying about, checking on supplies and plugging in curling irons, flat irons, blow-dryers, and hot rollers. I'd never seen so many people running around backstage at a fashion show—especially ten hours ahead of showtime. But then, this was no ordinary fashion show. *Still,* I thought, scanning the tables full of hair extensions, *this can't all be for Jamie Lee and me.*

Just then one of the casting directors handed me a pink-and-white-striped robe and escorted me to one of the lit makeup stations. It was time to become Angel-fied. Jamie Lee was already eyebrow-pencil deep in her own transformation at the other station, and my stylist was anxious to get started.

While we were having our makeup done, the director gave us a quick rundown of the day's activities.

"Once you get your preliminary hair and makeup done, we're going to shoot a couple of promo pieces with you and Heidi," she began. "I'd like a little footage of the two of you practicing your walks on the actual runway. Then we'll get some footage of both of you walking the actual runway. And you'll want to rock that piece, girls. It's the final challenge people will vote on." Jamie Lee and I shared a look of apprehensive excitement.

"Then," the director continued, "we'll get you retouched, put you in your looks for the evening, and get you runway ready for the final taping. We'll be running through the entire show twice tonight. Once at six o'clock, with just the talent, and then again at eight with the audience present. Jamie Lee, you'll be walking in the six o'clock show, and Kylie, you'll be walking in the eight o'clock. We'll edit in the footage of whoever wins the competition when the final show airs on December 1. Okay?"

Jamie Lee and I glanced at each other and then nodded.

After the director left, Jamie Lee looked at me in the mirror and said, "It makes sense, you know, for you to walk in the eight o'clock show." She smiled weakly and said, "Congrats."

I wasn't sure what to say. The fact that Jamie Lee was walking in the tech rehearsal and I was walking in the live show didn't mean that I'd won. The media challenge we'd shot two days ago hadn't even aired yet, and the audience wouldn't vote on our final runway walks for another two weeks.

"Thanks," I said. But I wasn't so sure she was right.

I had to admit, though, it would be a lot easier having a live audience to react to when I had my moment in the sun. Then, just as my stomach was beginning to tingle with nerves, Heidi appeared.

"Hello, ladies." She smiled broadly. "Congratulations on making the final two. I'm so excited for both of you."

My insides were trembling. Heidi was just as lovely in person as she was on-screen, and she had a smile that could light up an amphitheater.

"As soon as you're finished here, we're going to tape some quick promos, okay?" She looked at the stylists. "Are they ready?"

"Yep," they said, almost in unison. At once our makeup bibs were off and we were out of our chairs.

"All right, then." Heidi beamed. "Let's hit it!"

Holy cow. My mind raced as I followed Heidi to where the film crew was setting up. *I can't believe I'm actually going to be on television with Heidi Klum! Please, Lord, don't let me mess this up.*

After Jamie Lee and I were positioned on each side of Heidi, we went through a series of teasers that would run during the final show. Most were painfully simple. All we had to do was stand next to Heidi, smiling, while she said something along the lines of "And next will be our elimination results. Will it be Kylie or Jamie Lee?" It was that final sentence that set my nerves on edge.

"Okay, girls," the director said. "Now we're going to film two different scenarios. In the first one, we're going to have Heidi announce that Jamie Lee has won the title of Runway Angel, and then we'll do another one where she announces that Kylie has won. Try to react accordingly."

React accordingly? I thought. I mean, I got it, but seriously? How exactly do you react to the news that your lifelong goal has just come true? Or worse, that it hasn't?

I was still pondering how to respond when I heard Heidi's voice.

"The voting lines are now closed. The results are in. Either Jamie Lee or Kylie is about to set foot on our runway and become the winner of the Victoria's Secret Model Search 2009."

Then she turned and looked at the two of us. "You both did a fantastic job, but only one of you can get this prize. America, you've made your decision. The winner of the 2009 Victoria's Secret Runway Angel competition is . . ." And finally, after a dramatic pause: "Kylie!"

The fact that Heidi did the teasers out of order caught me off guard, and it was just the jolt that I needed to react . . . *accordingly*. I let out a quick, high-pitched scream, and without thinking, I leaped forward and threw my arms around Heidi's neck. Realizing what I'd done, I quickly took a step back, where Jamie Lee was waiting to give me a hug and graciously congratulate me.

"Okay, great," the director said, snapping me back to reality. "Now let's reset and shoot it again with Jamie Lee." With my heart still racing in my chest, I tried to calm myself and get ready to celebrate Jamie Lee's big news. Being a pro, Heidi re-created her lines perfectly, concluding with an identical dramatic pause before announcing, "Jamie Lee!"

Watching Jamie Lee react with such excitement, jumping and squealing enthusiastically before covering her mouth with her hands and stepping forward to hug Heidi, I found it surprisingly easy to smile and be happy for her. When she turned to me, I offered her a genuine hug. I really did like Jamie Lee. She had been sweet to me throughout the competition—something I especially appreciated in an industry where genuine kindness is hard to come by.

With the promos finished, Heidi gave us both quick hugs, wished us luck, and headed to her dressing room to get ready for the show. I was a little surprised to learn that Heidi was the only Angel who had her own private dressing room. Not even the other superstars in the mix that night—including Miranda Kerr, Doutzen Kroes, and Marisa Miller—had that privilege. But as one of the first and longest-reigning Angels, having dominated the industry for more than a decade, she'd earned it. As far as I'd come over the past few weeks, I still had a long way to go. I was about to find out if I'd take the next step.

"All right, ladies," the director said, gesturing toward the stage. "It's challenge time."

Without a moment to catch our breath following the agony and the ecstasy of the reaction shots, Jamie Lee and I were escorted to the runway to film our final challenge: the walk.

Just as I was starting to wonder which Angel would be

coaching us on the most important runway walk of our lives, statuesque Brazilian beauty Alessandra Ambrosio stepped out from behind the curtain, looking stunning in a black sequined dress. Standing there in a T-shirt and jeans, I suddenly felt horrifically underdressed—and very jittery.

"Hello, girls," she said with a smile. "Nervous?"

"A little," I responded, wondering if Alessandra and Jamie Lee could hear my heart pounding.

"Well, I know both of you have been practicing your walks all week," she began as the camera crews moved into position. "You need to have a lot of energy for this show. Millions of people will be watching you, and you've got to work every camera in the room. But the most important thing is to be sexy. This is Victoria's Secret, after all." She winked at us.

"So," she said, gesturing toward Jamie Lee, "show me what you've got."

I could tell Jamie Lee was nervous as she started down the runway. Maybe Alessandra thought so, too, because she didn't make any comments—not during Jamie Lee's walk and not after she'd finished. She just nodded and smiled.

"Okay, your turn," Alessandra said to me. I took a deep breath and started strutting down the runway, working my hips, blowing kisses, and pointing my finger at the imaginary crowd, just the way I'd seen Alessandra, Marisa, and Miranda do in past fashion shows.

When I got back to Alessandra, her eyes were wide. "You've been practicing," she said. "That was really fierce."

Fierce? I thought, a little surprised. *I'll take that.*

"Thank you, ladies," she continued. "I'll see you tonight. And good luck to you both." With that she departed, and so did the camera crew.

The promos were finished. The final challenge was completed. Now it was time to get ready for the show.

As Jamie Lee and I headed backstage to finish getting ready, all the other models had their turns getting plucked and pulled in every direction. Like cars on an assembly line, models moved from one station to the next, getting manicures, pedicures, spray tans, and full-body makeup, followed by extensive airbrushing to cover up any blemishes, scars, or visible cellulite and to bring out the definition of shoulders, arms, thighs, and abs. Then every Angel was fitted with three, sometimes four, rows of hair extensions, false eyelashes, and layer upon layer of mascara, eye shadow, lip liner, brow liner, blush—the works.

Wow, I marveled, slightly awestruck. *Who would have thought it would take so much time and work to make a Victoria's Secret model beautiful?*

When I watched the Fashion Show on TV as I was growing up, I just assumed the models naturally looked like that—with long, flowing hair; flawless, blemish-free skin; and bronzed, toned bodies. In short, I thought they were all perfect.

Huh, I mused, taking in the extraordinary transformations happening all around me. *So that's Victoria's secret.*

As the minutes ticked closer to the final call for the show, the activity backstage intensified. The Angels were getting fitted with their wings, which was no small task. Meanwhile, the Black Eyed Peas, who would be performing during the show, had arrived and were backstage schmoozing with the Angels.

I had just changed into the matching black-and-silver bra and panty set they'd given me, along with the sheer black jacket. The only thing left was the pair of red stilettos. After slipping into my heels, I took a step back and looked in the full-length mirror. I barely recognized myself, yet I couldn't stop smiling. They had done it. They had made me an Angel. Granted, it was eight hours and a roomful of beauty supplies later, but I was an Angel.

With only a few minutes to go before showtime, Ed Razek came backstage, thanked us for our hard work, and told us how proud he was of all of us. Then he popped open several bottles of champagne and started passing them around. As people made toasts to the show's success, I just held my glass in my hand. Then one of the other models raised her glass to toast with me and said, "Drink up! You'll have more fun out there if you're a little tipsy."

I smiled and took a sip, but I wasn't really interested in getting tipsy. Not only was I underage, but I also knew what the Bible said about getting drunk—in a nutshell, that it's unwise and makes you do stupid things. Besides, I wanted to be on top of my game when I made my first walk in a Victoria's Secret Fashion Show.

The show was in full swing, and I was trying to keep my nerves in check. From backstage I focused on one of the television monitors, watching the other models walk the runway. Each one of them was dazzling, and the wings created a stunning effect. The Black Eyed Peas were rocking the house, and the audience seemed to be loving every minute of the show. On the rare occasions the camera panned the crowd, I tried to find Mike. I knew he'd never attended anything like this, and I wasn't sure what he'd make of it. To the uninitiated, the Victoria's Secret Fashion Show can be a lot to take in.

Before I knew it, the stagehand was motioning for me to take my place at the entrance to the runway. As I crossed the room to take my mark, Heidi shot me an enormous smile.

"This is your stage," she told me. "Own it!"

I stood in the shadows for a brief moment, and then, on cue, I rounded the corner and hit the runway. As I walked into the lights, I could feel the music pulsing through my entire body. The crowd was going wild.

Their enthusiasm was infectious. The more they cheered and applauded, the more I worked that runway. I blew kisses, I waved, and I rocked my hips like never before. It was one of those surreal moments that seemed to pass both in slow motion and in the blink of an eye. Suddenly I was backstage, my hand at my chest as I tried to catch my breath. Meanwhile Alessandra, Doutzen, Miranda, and the others all hugged and congratulated me. It was one of the most exhilarating experiences of my life. I might not have been wearing wings that night, but I was definitely soaring.

When it was over, the backstage area turned into a celebration zone, with a small army of celebrities joining the Angels for champagne, hugs, kisses, and photo ops. As for me, I just wanted to find Mike. While it was exciting to see stars like Michael Bay, Jay-Z, Fergie, and Simon Le Bon up close, Mike was the only person I really wanted to celebrate with.

When I finally spotted Mike standing off to the side near one of the emergency exits, I kicked off my heels, broke into a sprint, and jumped in his arms.

"I'm so proud of you, baby," he said, giving me a kiss. "You were truly awesome out there."

I heaved a gigantic sigh of relief. His words of approval meant more to me than all the applause and congratulations I'd received that night.

After I changed, Mike and I took a cab downtown to the Pink Carpet after-party. When we arrived at the large nightclub, it was packed with celebrities, rock stars, supermodels, and famous athletes. Since Mike and I weren't into the club scene, I made sure I thanked Monica Mitro and Ed Razek for giving me the opportunity to walk in the show, and then Mike and I sneaked out the back and headed off for our own private celebration, complete with a massive dinner at one of my favorite Italian restaurants and a heaping bowl of coffee ice cream for dessert.

As I lay in bed that night, I thanked God for fulfilling a lifelong dream. Even if I never walked in another Victoria's Secret show, this was an evening I would remember for the rest of my life.

It was also an evening Mike would remember for the rest of *his* life. I wasn't the only one who had gotten a glimpse into what life as a Victoria's Secret Angel would look like. While Mike was doing his best to be a loving, supportive husband, he privately was struggling with the idea of having his wife parade around onstage in sexy lingerie while millions of men looked on and applauded.

As I drifted off that night dreaming of wings, Mike was on his knees, asking the Lord for wisdom—for both of us.

Chapter 22

BE CAREFUL WHAT YOU WISH FOR

We know that in all things God works for
the good of those who love him, who have
been called according to his purpose.

ROMANS 8:28

THE NEXT DAY Mike and I flew home to spend the Thanksgiving
holiday with our families, and I was glad to be getting out of New
York. Not only was I looking forward to seeing everyone, but it
would also be a nice distraction while I waited for the winner to
be announced. Mike and I would return to New York in a few
days for the moment of truth: the airing of the Fashion Show on
December 1.

Mike, my parents, and my in-laws did their best to keep my
mind off the competition, but I was barely able to think of anything
else. I spent the majority of the holiday online, frantically searching
for blogs, comments, or discussion posts related to the show, trying
to determine how the public was leaning—toward Jamie Lee or
me. By the time the weekend was over, I'd managed to squander

yet another precious holiday season with my family as a result of obsessing over my career.

By the time December 1 finally rolled around, I was pretty much a nervous wreck.

"Sweetie, you said yourself that it's all in God's hands now," Mike reminded me as I was getting dressed for the official viewing party.

"I know," I said. "I've just wanted this for so long, and I never imagined I'd actually get this close."

Still, Mike was right. It was in God's hands. I'd given it to Him in the very beginning, when Mike's stepmom handed me that entry form. Win or lose, it had been a phenomenal ride. And win or lose, I would still walk out of the club at the end of the night with the man of my dreams—and with memories that would last a lifetime.

"You ready?" Mike smiled at me and held out his hand.

I gave myself one last glance in the mirror, brushed a speck of lint off my jacket, and took a deep breath. Then I reached for Mike's hand. "Yep. For anything." *Please, God,* I prayed. *But only if it's Your will.*

By the time Mike and I arrived at The Box, a trendy club on the Lower East Side, the viewing party was already in full swing. Like the celebration following the competition, this party was packed with celebrities, Angels, supermodels, and paparazzi. True to form, Monica Mitro and Ed Razek were working the room—greeting guests and making sure the champagne was flowing freely.

Mike and I were feeling out of our element, so as soon as we spied Jamie Lee and her boyfriend sitting at a table off to the side, we walked over to join them. If anyone else knew how I was feeling right now, it was Jamie Lee. And competition aside, she had been a good friend to me throughout the entire experience.

"How are you holding up?" she asked as I took my seat.

"I'm a nervous wreck," I admitted with a laugh.

"Me, too," she said.

We did our best to make polite chitchat with the endless parade of well-wishers who stopped by our table to congratulate us and wish us luck, but ultimately it was all I could do to keep my nervous stomach in check.

Then the lights dimmed, and the giant screens lining the walls of the club filled with the words we'd been waiting for: *The 2009 Victoria's Secret Fashion Show.* My heart leaped into my throat, and I clasped Mike's hand so tightly I'm surprised I didn't break a few of his fingers.

For the next forty-five minutes my eyes were glued to the screen. The show was everything a Victoria's Secret Fashion Show is meant to be—elaborate, sexy, over the top. Every time they showed one of the teasers with Heidi, Jamie Lee, and me, the crowd in the club went crazy, which was pretty surreal in itself, considering we were pretty much the only people in the club who weren't celebrities.

Finally the moment arrived. Jamie Lee and I shot each other one last nervous smile, and then we looked at Heidi's face on the screen. The words she was about to utter would change one of our lives forever.

"The voting lines are now closed," Heidi said. "The results are in. Either Jamie Lee or Kylie is about to set foot on our runway and become the winner of the Victoria's Secret Model Search 2009."

I held my breath as Mike's grip tightened around my hand.

"America, you've made your decision," Heidi continued. "The winner of the 2009 Victoria's Secret Runway Angel competition is . . . Kylie!"

The club exploded with cheers, and flashbulbs lit up the room.

Mike grabbed me and hugged tight. "You did it, baby! I'm so proud of you!"

Unable to find my voice, I clung to Mike, trembling with excitement.

Thank You, God. Thank You so much, I prayed as tears brimmed in my eyes.

When I looked up, I saw Jamie Lee with her face in her hands, her shoulders shaking. Her boyfriend was at her side, trying to console her.

Oh, poor Jamie Lee, I thought.

"Mike, let's go over there so Jamie Lee can have a few moments in private." I felt terrible. Here I was celebrating, when right beside me Jamie Lee was feeling the weight of her dreams crashing around her. I wanted to say something, but in that moment I was afraid it would only make things worse. So Mike and I quietly moved to the opposite end of the room, taking the chaos with us.

Ed Razek made his way over to greet us. "Congratulations, Kylie!" he said, giving me a kiss on the cheek. "I'm so happy for you. We all are. And we're really looking forward to working with you."

"Thank you," I said, feeling completely overwhelmed. "I'm still in shock." I laughed nervously. "I'm so grateful to you and Ms. Mitro and everyone at Victoria's Secret for giving me this opportunity."

"Enjoy the night, Kylie." A broad smile broke across his face. "You've earned it."

This is it, I thought. *No more roach-infested apartments, no more pot-smoking roommates, no more test shoots, no more casting agents harping about my weight.* I had officially broken in. I had hit the big time. *Everything is going to be different now,* I thought.

And then the evening took a turn I never expected.

Suddenly the lights dimmed, and out of nowhere, nude burlesque dancers appeared and started doing unspeakable things onstage. Having grown up in Las Vegas, I'm not easily shocked. But this was so far beyond anything in my frame of reference that my mind could barely take in what I was seeing. All around us people were bumping and grinding, and some of the Victoria's Secret models were whistling at the dancers and cheering them on. What was even more surprising, however, was the fact that aside from Mike and me, nobody seemed to find any of it remotely inappropriate.

"Kylie," Mike said, pulling me aside, "I don't want to be around all this stuff. You do what you have to do, and when you're done, I'll be out front waiting for you, okay?"

I'd never seen him look so uncomfortable, and I was mortified. I couldn't believe I'd put him in this situation. I couldn't believe *I* was in this situation.

"I'm so sorry, Mike." My throat was burning, and tears started to form in my eyes. "You go ahead. I'll be out in a minute. I promise." I was feeling guiltier by the second.

As Mike made his way out of the club, I stood frozen to my spot. My heart was racing, and my hands were trembling. I suddenly felt light headed, and I was sure I was going to be sick.

I have to get out of here, I thought. I made one last sweep through the club, thanking the other Victoria's Secret bigwigs and the Angels for everything they'd done for me, while staying as far away from the stage as I possibly could. Then, satisfied that I'd made enough of an appearance not to be missed, I grabbed my coat and slipped out the back. The most exciting night of my career had lasted all of eight minutes before everything fell apart.

When I came around the side of the club, I saw Mike standing off to the side, shivering in the cold. I rushed over to him and hugged him as tightly as I could. The tears I'd been struggling to hold back started flowing.

"I am so sorry," I said over and over.

"It's okay, Ky. Let's just try to forget about it."

But it wasn't okay, and I couldn't forget about it.

"I don't understand," I cried into Mike's shoulder. "Why would God let me win this competition if this is what it's going to be like?"

"I don't know, baby," Mike said. "We just have to trust that God has a plan. Don't forget that the Bible says God uses all things for good."

I knew he was right, but at that moment I was having a hard time seeing how any of the things going on inside that club could be used for good.

Maybe this party was just a one-time thing, I reasoned. *I'm sure everything will be better from here on out. It has to be.*

Things didn't get better. In fact, it was all downhill from there.

Later that evening, I received an e-mail from one of the bigwigs at Victoria's Secret that literally turned my stomach. Apparently one of the celebrities at the after-party thought I was his type, and this exec wanted to know if it was okay for him to pass along my phone number so we could "get together."

You've got to be kidding me, I thought. I'd mentioned Mike in practically every interview, and I'd made a point of wearing my wedding ring throughout the entire competition. *I even introduced Mike to this guy tonight!* I marveled. *How in the world could he possibly think this was okay?*

I had heard that the owners encouraged the Angels to date celebrities because of the extra publicity it provided. I knew, for example, that Gisele Bündchen had dated Leonardo DiCaprio for years before marrying Tom Brady, that Heidi Klum was married to Seal, and that Miranda Kerr was with Orlando Bloom. But since I was happily married, I assumed they realized I was off the market.

Clearly, though, the fact that I had a husband didn't make a bit of difference in their minds. And clearly Mike wasn't famous enough for their taste.

I immediately responded with a gracious yet firm message that read, "I am very flattered, but I am completely in love with my husband. Thank you, Kylie."

That night, as I settled into bed, my mind was swirling with emotions. After years of hard work, failures, and disappointments, I finally had achieved my life's dream. So why did I suddenly feel like I was stuck in a nightmare?

Mike was doing his best to be supportive, but I could tell he was upset. I was having a hard time brushing off everything that had happened—the X-rated party scene, my new bosses trying to fix me up with a more "Angel-worthy" partner, and all the alcohol people kept pushing in my face, even though they knew I still was well underage.

I'd been in the industry long enough to know how morally bankrupt it could be—the drugs, the nudity, the sex—but I always figured that once you reached a certain level—*this level*—things would be different. So why wasn't it?

And yet I knew that Mike was right. I believed God had a plan for my life, and for some reason He had allowed me to win this competition. People make mistakes. God doesn't. Whatever the divine reasoning, I had been given this opportunity, and I was going to make the best of it.

Okay, I reasoned. *I'll just focus on the modeling and ignore all the peripheral craziness. I can still be a Christian and a supermodel at the same time.*

I had no idea just how impossible that was going to be.

Chapter 23

DÉJÀ VU

No one can serve two masters. For you will
hate one and love the other; you will be
devoted to one and despise the other.

MATTHEW 6:24, NLT

I AWOKE THE NEXT MORNING to a completely different reality, having gone from virtual anonymity to superstar status—literally overnight. When I logged on to Mike's laptop to check my e-mail, I was stunned to discover that I was the number one Googled person in the world and had received more than five thousand new friend requests on Facebook. On top of that, my in-box was overflowing with requests for interviews, special appearances, and photo ops. There was also a note from Ed Razek inviting me to St. Barts for the upcoming Victoria's Secret swimsuit catalog shoot.

The swimsuit catalog, I thought. *Mom will die when she hears this.* When I picked up my phone to call her, I discovered dozens of messages from elite modeling agencies all over the country that wanted to meet with me . . . at my convenience.

Wow, I marveled. *What a difference a pair of wings makes.*

❧

Though I hated the idea of being away from Mike, especially in the wake of the after-party fiasco, we really didn't have any other choice. My career was starting to take off in New York, and he needed to get back to the West Coast for a series of business meetings. We were about to face our first post-competition challenge—surviving a bicoastal relationship.

"It'll be fine," Mike reassured me as he got out of the cab at the airport. "You just do what you need to do, and I'll fly back out here as soon as I can." He kissed me good-bye and, just before he went through the revolving doors, turned and said, "We'll be together again before you know it!"

But when? I lamented, thinking about my packed schedule. I had dozens of appearances scheduled before Christmas. And right after that, I was due to leave for St. Barts. Mike and I had been married barely six months, and we'd spent a third of that time apart while I was in the competition. Now we were facing yet another separation.

Having lost sight of Mike in the crowd, I reluctantly got into the cab and headed back to Manhattan. Thankfully, though, I wasn't alone in this vast city. Mike's stepsister, Mason, had flown to New York to be my makeup artist for all my events. I was glad to have her around—especially as the craziness amped up even more.

Everywhere I went in New York, somebody recognized me. It was fun at first—signing autographs and having pictures taken—but the novelty wore off quickly, and I grew tired of always having to be "on," always having to be camera ready.

Being low key by nature, I was accustomed to schlepping around in jeans or sweatpants, without makeup and with my hair shoved under a baseball cap. Not anymore. With fans of the show and paparazzi lurking around every corner, waiting to snap a quick photo, I had to get "Angel-fied" every day. I wasn't just Kylie Bisutti anymore. I was essentially the property of Victoria's Secret, and I had an image to uphold.

The long blonde extensions I'd worn in the Fashion Show became permanent fixtures in my overprocessed, artificially colored hair. I started getting spray tans once a week, and I never left the hotel without a fully made-up face, false eyelashes, and a sexy outfit. Some might call it glamorous, but for me it was simply exhausting.

So was my schedule. December went by in a blur of parties and premieres. Mike was able to fly in for a few of them, but for the most part it was just Mason and me. For an introvert like me, this schedule made for a lot of long, lonely—and at times uncomfortable—evenings.

Before I knew it, it was time to leave for St. Barts. *Finally,* I thought, *a little downtime with some of the other models. Maybe they could give me some advice on how to handle all the craziness.*

I couldn't figure out how anyone could keep up this type of pace—especially the Angels who were married with kids. I was only a month in, and I already felt like I was drowning.

There has to be a secret to making this bearable, I thought.

The resort in St. Barts was nothing short of spectacular. After spending the better part of the past three months freezing in New York, I was looking forward to taking a relaxing stroll along the beach, eating a light dinner, and then going straight to bed so I'd be at my best for the morning's shoot. But the rest of the girls had other plans—namely, a gigantic, calorie-laden dinner, followed by dancing and drinks at a local club. *Not another club,* I thought. *Don't these people ever sleep?*

Apparently not, because the party rolled on late into the evening, with the complimentary drinks flowing and the cigarette smoke filling the air.

"Here you go, Kylie," one of the other Angels said, handing me a colorful umbrella-topped drink. "Drink up!"

I smiled politely and thanked her, but I just held the drink in my hand all night, casually spilling out a little every now and then so it would seem like I was drinking it.

This is ridiculous, I thought, checking my watch and doing a mental countdown to our photo shoot, which was now only a few hours away. I felt like a kid in high school, desperately trying to fit in with the cool girls at the party but failing miserably.

After watching the other models drink and smoke and flirt with the guys at the bar for a while, I finally spied a few of the hair and makeup people sitting at a quiet table off to the side, so I went over and talked with them.

I wish Doutzen were here, I thought. She'd been kind to me during the competition, and I was looking forward to spending some time with her. Unfortunately, though, her flight out of Amsterdam had been delayed, so she wouldn't be arriving until early the next morning.

It was becoming evident that the gap between the other models and me was more significant than I'd originally anticipated. For me, having fun meant a relaxing evening of watching movies and playing board games with my family. For them, it meant drinking until dawn and flirting with total strangers at a noisy club.

I could work the runway and play to the camera with the best of them, but I thought once the cameras were put away and the crowds went home, we could just kick back, relax, and be ourselves. But I was discovering that the sexy, flirty Victoria's Secret persona that ruled the runway was expected to carry over after hours as well—especially in public settings. It was all part of the package, part of the fantasy.

Being an Angel wasn't just a job; it was a lifestyle. And I was both expected and being paid to play along.

Fortunately, the makeup crew decided to cut out early, and they offered me a lift back to the hotel, which I gladly accepted. Once I got to my room, I called Mike. Even four time zones away, it was pretty late, so he knew something was amiss before I even said anything.

"Kylie? What's wrong?" he asked, sounding a bit groggy.

What's wrong? I thought. *Everything.* But since he already sounded worried—not to mention tired—I decided not to give him a detailed description of the evening's events.

"I'm fine," I said. "The resort is beautiful. I just wish you were here, that's all. I miss you."

"I miss you, too, sweetie," he said. "Why do you sound so sad?"

Apparently I wasn't sounding very convincing, so I decided to let it all out.

"I just don't fit in. I'm the only one here who doesn't smoke or get drunk and dance on tables, and . . ." I paused to collect my thoughts. "Being a Victoria's Secret Angel just isn't what I thought it would be."

"I'm sorry, Kylie," he said. "I know how much it meant to you to become an Angel. I'm praying for you, sweetie. Every day."

I knew it was true. Mike had been praying for me since that first photo shoot aired on CBS and the entire country saw me Photoshopped to three times my normal cup size. I wasn't the only one in this marriage who was feeling conflicted about this crazy world we'd been plunged into.

Mike knew this had been my dream since I was a little girl, and he knew how hard I'd worked to get here. But he was also starting to see that eventually this lifestyle would cause some serious problems in my relationship with the Lord. I simply couldn't live the lifestyle the brand demanded *and* be a strong, faithful Christian wife. Mike knew it. And he was praying with all his heart that I would come to realize it too. And soon.

The next day was picture perfect—the ideal setting for a swimsuit shoot. When I arrived at the site, my mood was lifted when I saw that Doutzen had arrived. Even better, she and I had been paired for the shoot.

Doutzen was a true professional. Besides that, just watching her pose was a learning experience for me. She knew how to work a photo shoot better than almost any model I'd seen. She made the entire process look effortless.

Following Doutzen's lead, I turned in one of the best photo shoots of my life that morning. The photographer loved what I did, and I was reminded that I really did love the technical aspect of modeling. I just wished all the other stuff didn't have to go with it.

I returned from the St. Barts shoot with a renewed sense of confidence in my modeling abilities and an even firmer resolve to find a way to strike a balance between the job I loved and my allegiance to God and my husband. *I just have to be stronger when it comes to avoiding uncomfortable situations,* I reasoned. *I can still be a model; I just won't go to the clubs or bars with the others. I don't care what they think. As long as I keep doing great work, the jobs will come.*

After talking with Mike and visiting with several of the top modeling agencies in New York, I decided to sign with IMG, which is widely regarded as the best modeling agency in the world. The fact that they also represented Heidi Klum, Gisele Bündchen, and Miranda Kerr cemented my decision.

Surprisingly, as soon as I signed, they asked me to go out and do a series of test shoots, much like I'd done for Envy and Red several years ago. *Seriously?* I thought. *What could possibly be missing from my portfolio?* Still, they were the best in the business, and I was anxious to get off on the right foot, so I agreed to the bookings.

Before I headed off for the test shoots, I met with IMG's hair and makeup people. There was something about the way they kept staring at my hair and furtively whispering to one another that gave me a sinking feeling in the pit of my stomach.

"Okay, so here's what we think," the master stylist finally said, stepping forward and running his fingers through my extension-enhanced blonde tresses. "We want to go more one-color with fewer highlights for these test shoots."

Since I'd just had my hair lightened three weeks earlier for the St. Barts shoot, I was a little concerned about coloring it again so soon. That much processing can be extremely damaging, and I couldn't help but feel as though the stakes were higher now that I'd crossed into A-list territory. I decided to aim for a compromise.

"If we have to color it," I said, "I'd really like to use my own stylist here in New York, since she knows what's been done to it over the past few weeks. Would that be okay?"

"Oh, heavens, no," the stylist said, sounding offended. "We only use our own hair people here at IMG. Don't worry," he continued. "We're just going to make your hair a little richer—you'll love it."

As it turned out, I had reason to worry. By the time they were finished, my beautifully highlighted caramel locks were a sickly orange red. It was atrocious. *This looks even worse than the jet-black dye job they did on me in Thailand,* I thought. *At this level, shouldn't they be better at this?* I did my best to put on a brave face in front of my new employers, but as soon as I walked outside, the tears spilled over. Sure, it was only hair, but it was *my* hair. And I hated it. How was I supposed to exude any sense of confidence in my test shoot looking like this?

The next day, as requested, I did the test shoot. But the minute it was over, I went straight to my own stylist for an emergency intervention. *I don't care what IMG says,* I thought. *I'm not walking around New York looking like Bozo the Clown.* On the plus side, at least I wasn't being recognized on the street anymore.

Fortunately my stylist was able to tone down the brass and make me more of a strawberry blonde with caramel lowlights. And thank goodness, because I had another test shoot scheduled for the following day.

"You're just going to love this photographer," my new booker gushed.

I winced. *That's what you guys said about the dye job.*

"He's incredibly artsy," he continued. "Very avant-garde. Here's his address." He handed me a slip of paper. "He shoots in his apartment in Brooklyn."

In his apartment? My mind immediately flashed back to the last photographer who had done a test shoot in his apartment: the Saran Wrap creep. I had a bad feeling about this. Fortunately Mike was in town, so just to be on the safe side, I asked him to go with me. History had already repeated itself once with the dye job. I wasn't about to let it happen twice in one week.

The second Mike and I walked into the photographer's apartment, my worst fears were confirmed—there were nude photographs covering the walls. In the industry, it's called art. In my mind, it's called pornography. Mike and I froze in the doorway. Neither of us knew what to say. I glanced nervously at Mike. His eyes were squeezed shut, and his hand closed even tighter around mine. I thought he was merely averting his gaze from the photographs around him, but in actuality, he was praying feverishly—for patience, for strength, for wisdom, for my safety.

"You must be Kylie," the photographer said. "And this is?" He motioned toward Mike.

"This is my husband, Mike." I was still holding firmly to Mike's hand.

"Oh." A look of surprise washed over his face. He reached out to shake Mike's hand, but Mike just gripped mine even tighter and looked right through him.

The photographer instinctively took a step back and then, with his eyes darting between the two of us, asked, "So, Mike . . . will you be staying?"

Mike closed his eyes and took a deep breath. "No. I think I'll wait outside."

I tried to get a read on Mike's expression, but his face looked completely blank. When he turned to look at me, I saw the hurt in his eyes. "I'll be right outside this door," he said protectively.

I nodded. There was so much I wanted to say, but all I was able to manage as he turned to leave was, "I'm so sorry, Mike."

It was the second time in our marriage Mike had needed to walk away from a compromising situation I'd put him in. And once again, I stayed behind . . . alone. I felt terrible.

"All right then!" the photographer exclaimed, clapping his hands. "Shall we get started?"

"Yeah," I replied weakly. "I guess so."

As much as I was dreading this shoot, I didn't want to do anything that would upset IMG right off the bat, and I knew walking away from a test shoot they'd arranged would not go over well. *Just focus on the shoot, ignore the pictures, and get out of here,* I told myself.

"You know, you have a great body," the photographer said, giving me the once-over. There was a time when a compliment like that would have been an incredible ego boost, but now, with my husband standing dejected in the hall, I just felt cheap and ashamed. "There's a swimsuit in the bathroom. Go ahead and put that on."

I let out a sigh of relief. *Oh, good,* I thought. *A swimsuit shot. Maybe this won't be so bad after all.*

I couldn't have been more wrong.

Waiting for me in the bathroom was a white bathing suit that was so sheer it was practically the equivalent of posing nude.

"This is really see through," I said, voicing my concern from the bathroom.

"No worries," he replied nonchalantly. "I can Photoshop out anything that looks too vulgar."

Then why can't we use a less vulgar suit to begin with? I wondered. Of course, given the photos that lined his apartment walls, I had a suspicion that our interpretations of *vulgar* differed immensely.

When I came out of the bathroom, my arms were crossed self-consciously in front of me.

"Don't worry," he assured me again. "I promise, I'll go back over these to make sure nothing shows through." Having been duped before, I was dubious, but because he came so highly recommended from IMG, I decided to trust him. That was my second mistake. The first had been not following Mike out of the apartment to begin with.

I don't think I'd ever been as uncomfortable or self-conscious during a photo shoot as I was that afternoon. Photoshop or not, just knowing what this guy was seeing while Mike was in the hall was almost too much for me to bear.

There was no question in my mind: nothing about this shoot felt right. But if I walked out now, I was afraid it would spell the end of my modeling career. Nobody in the industry would want to work with a model labeled difficult or prudish—especially not Victoria's Secret. *God allowed me to win that competition for a reason,* I thought. *I just wish I knew what it was.*

There was no hiding the fact that Mike was upset about the photo shoot. He may not have known very much about the modeling industry, but he knew that what had transpired in the photographer's apartment was wrong. And on some level, I did too. But in my mind, Mike had the option of walking out. I didn't. *It's not his career at stake,* I rationalized.

But it wasn't my career Mike was worried about; it was my walk with Christ. And every time I compromised what I believed for the sake of my career, or put my modeling reputation ahead of my relationships with Mike and God, the values I stood for were becoming less and less clear. And things were about to get even murkier.

⌘

Anxious to get away from the frenetic pace of New York, Mike and I returned to Los Angeles to spend some much-needed downtime with family and with each other. With the craziness of the past few months, we'd barely had a chance to establish ourselves as a married couple, and we were looking forward to a little bit of normalcy.

One afternoon I was updating my Facebook page and decided to Google my name to see if Victoria's Secret had released any teaser images from the swimsuit catalog. There were swimsuit images up there, all right—but they weren't from St. Barts. Instead, I saw an entire listing of porn sites advertising, "See Kylie Bisutti—NUDE!" I clicked on the first link and watched in horror as one image after another of me in the see-through bathing suit from the Brooklyn shoot appeared. They weren't retouched at all, and you could see absolutely everything. I felt sick to my stomach.

"Mike!" I yelled.

"What?" he called, rushing into the room. "What's wrong?"

I was already crying uncontrollably. "Do you remember that shoot in Brooklyn?" I choked out. "The photographer uploaded all those shots onto porn sites!"

Mike's eyes widened in shock. "You've got to be kidding me." His voice was shaking. "How could this happen?"

"Those pictures were only supposed to be for my book!" I sobbed. "And he promised he'd Photoshop over the parts I didn't want shown. Now any time someone Googles my name, this will come up!" My stomach churned as I recalled how high my Google ranking had been since I'd won the competition two months before. "What am I going to do?" I wailed.

Mike grabbed his phone. "I'm calling our attorney." His face flushed with rage. "We're going to make sure that guy never does another photo shoot again, and we're going to make sure those pictures are taken down immediately."

While Mike stormed into the next room to speak with our attorney, I sat there alone, feeling betrayed and helpless.

I decided to call IMG and tell them what had happened. After my words finally tumbled out, I was shocked to discover how unfazed they were.

"Kylie, we can't control what happens with the images of you," my agent said. "Most of the Victoria's Secret girls have lingerie pictures on sites like that. If you're going to pose wearing sexy things, those images will likely end up on provocative sites."

What have I done? I lamented. *I knew the second I set foot in the apartment that it was a bad idea. Why didn't I just leave with Mike? Why didn't I trust my gut?*

I'd learned back in my youth group days that our consciences are God's way of telling us what's right and what's wrong. God had been telling me to walk away that day. I'd heard Him loud and clear—I just hadn't listened. And now I was suffering the consequences.

Millions of people have access to these pictures! My head was pounding by now. *And there's nothing I can do about it.*

I wished a giant crack would open in the ground and swallow me whole. I had humiliated my husband, destroyed my reputation, and embarrassed my family—all for the sake of pleasing my new agency and keeping up my new supermodel status. For the next several days I hid out at the house, too ashamed to see anyone—including my family. I could barely look Mike in the eye.

I'm trying to do what's right, God, I prayed silently. *I had no idea this would happen. I just want to do my job, and I want my family to be proud of me. So why do all these horrible things keep happening?*

The answer was right in front of me—it was so close I could have reached out and touched it. I just needed one last push.

As devastating as the past week had been, I couldn't hide forever. Shortly after the infamous photo shoot, I had booked a spread with *Maxim*, a popular men's magazine that had profiled a number of Angels over the years. It seemed like a great opportunity to be launched as the newest face of Victoria's Secret. Still reeling from the whole debacle with the swimsuit photos, I saw it as an opportunity to reestablish myself as a legitimate and respectable model in the industry.

In light of recent events, Mike had insisted on accompanying me to the shoot, and I was glad that he did. I was still feeling pretty apprehensive about jumping back into the fray, and having him there helped set my mind and my nerves at ease.

Once again they wanted me to model swimwear—only this time the suit was completely opaque. I breathed a sigh of relief, but Mike still seemed troubled.

"It's okay, Mike," I said. "You can't see through this one at all." But there was something deeper at stake, and both of us knew it.

"Okay, Kylie," the photographer said. "We're ready for you."

Drawing on what I'd learned from watching Doutzen in St. Barts, I put forth my very best effort, and the shoot started off beautifully. After I did some poolside shots, the photographer asked how I felt about doing some pictures in the water.

"Sure," I said, easing myself into the pool.

After a few more shots, the photographer said the three magic words—"That's a wrap"—so I climbed out of the pool and draped myself in a towel. I told Mike I'd be only a few more minutes, and then I went inside to change.

I felt worlds better. The shoot had gone extremely well, and not one person on the set had even mentioned the Internet fiasco.

Mike, on the other hand, was uncharacteristically quiet on the drive home.

"What's wrong, babe?" I asked. "You seem like you're upset about something."

He stared ahead quietly for a few seconds before responding. "You looked really beautiful today."

"Thanks," I said cheerily.

"That's not what I meant, Ky," he continued. "Guys are going to have those pictures of you hanging on their walls. They're going to be staring at you all the time, thinking . . ." He paused for a second. "Who knows what they'll be thinking."

"But, babe, that's just how guys are," I reasoned. "It doesn't matter if I'm in an old pair of sweats at Starbucks or in a bikini on the cover of *Maxim*. They're still going to stare at me. What's the difference?"

Mike looked as if he wanted to say more but after a moment seemed to change his mind. Then he sighed and turned on the radio.

I don't get it, I thought.

And maybe, at the end of the day, that was the problem.

Chapter 24

THE LAST PUSH

Do not love the world or anything in the world.
If anyone loves the world, love for the Father is
not in them. For everything in the world—he lust
of the flesh, the lust of the eyes, and the pride of life—
comes not from the Father but from the world.
The world and its desires pass away, but whoever
does the will of God lives forever.

I JOHN 2:15-17

LITTLE BY LITTLE, I started to feel like a wedge was being driven between Mike and me, and I wasn't sure how to fix it. I knew he was bothered by the fact that men found my pictures provocative. But every time I tried to explain that this was just the way modeling worked and that there was nothing I could do about it, it seemed to make matters worse.

The problem was, there *was* something I could do about it. I just wasn't ready to accept it yet. And as much as Mike wanted to tell me what to do, he knew it was a realization I needed to come to on my own. So while I continued to stumble blindly along the path of destruction, Mike kept praying that the Lord would open my eyes to the truth.

Meanwhile, I attended more red-carpet affairs and went to

a couple of exclusive Victoria's Secret events, including an autograph signing for Victoria's Secret at their store in Chicago. The job offers continued to pour in too—notably, a cover shoot for *FHM*. Like *Maxim*, I knew *FHM* was a predominantly image-driven magazine that catered to an adult male audience, and while it certainly wasn't on par with *Playboy* or *Penthouse*, there was no mistaking its intent. The models featured in it were there for one reason and one reason only—to entice men. And now that I was a Victoria's Secret Angel, that was right at the top of my job description.

Mike had a business meeting the morning of the shoot, so I had to go alone. Since the *Maxim* shoot had gone so smoothly, I wasn't overly concerned. Besides, Mike was always so uncomfortable in these situations, and I figured being on my own might help me loosen up a little. Even though I was used to posing for spreads like this, I became decidedly self-conscious whenever I did so in front of Mike. The fact that I never pieced together why is beyond me. But the truth is, nobody knows how to blur the distinction between right and wrong like the enemy.

The shoot took place in a beautiful mansion in the heart of Beverly Hills. After getting my hair and makeup done, I was led upstairs to the master bedroom, where I would be posing in a variety of lingerie sets, ranging from soft, frilly lace to more provocative black leather.

Looking at the selections I'd be wearing that day, I knew Mike wouldn't be happy. But this was *FHM*. Models and movie stars all over the world would kill for this opportunity. *Besides*, I reasoned, *I can't help what other men think.* Unfortunately, I was so blinded by my own ambition that it never occurred to me that at the very least I could have helped what Mike thought.

"Okay, darlin'," the photographer called from the balcony. "Let's get started."

Darlin'? I thought. *That's getting a little personal.* But then again, I was about to spend several hours posing for him in some fairly risqué lingerie, so I guess I couldn't really complain.

We started with some simple shots out on the balcony, taking advantage of the morning light filtering softly through the trees. Then we moved indoors for some shots of me lounging around the suite and sitting on the edge of the enormous marble tub in the master bath. As much as I tried to relax and get into the shoot, though, I couldn't stop thinking about Mike and how he'd react when these pictures hit the newsstands and the web. Apparently, my apprehension showed.

"Come on, sweetheart." The photographer was starting to sound slightly exasperated. "Loosen up. Have some fun with this."

But I wasn't having fun. As we got further into the shoot, the lingerie became more revealing and the poses grew more suggestive. The more the photographer tried to get me to loosen up, the tenser I became. And the more uptight I became, the more frustrated and aggressive he became in return.

By the time the shoot moved to the bed, we had both reached our breaking points.

"Okay, look." By now he wasn't even trying to hide the irritation in his voice. "I want you to climb into bed and hold up the covers like you don't have any panties on. Do you think you can do that?"

Fighting back tears and trying to block the image of Mike's face from my mind, I attempted to do what the photographer asked. But I couldn't do it. All of a sudden, it didn't feel like just another photo shoot. It felt *wrong*. I didn't feel sexy or beautiful anymore. I only felt dirty, embarrassed, and ashamed.

His anger boiling over, the photographer dropped his camera at his side and glared at me. Then, in front of the entire light and makeup crew, he yelled, "What's the matter with you? You are ruining this shoot! You're a Victoria's Secret model, for Christ's sake—this is your job! Don't you want to be like Gisele? This is what you get paid for."

That's when it finally hit me. I was being paid to tease, tempt, and tantalize men. And it wasn't just my job. As a Victoria's Secret Angel, I was expected to make this my whole identity. And it colored the way everyone in the industry—and in the world—viewed me.

It had taken long enough for the epiphany to hit. I'd known for years that a big part of the industry was selling sex—especially when it came to lingerie. But until I heard him say the words, "This is what you get paid for," it had never really hit home before.

I felt sick to my stomach. There was only one type of woman I knew of who sold sex for a living, and the idea that people all over the world might be casting me in that light made me physically ill. As I sat there hugging my knees to my chest, shaking with anger and shame, a myriad of images from the past three years raced through my mind—the seedy Saran Wrap photographer, the ridiculously altered Grand Central Station shot, the sexy runway walk Victoria's Secret expected, the other Angels bumping and grinding with the burlesque dancers at the after-party, the partying in St. Barts, the see-through bathing suit, the porn sites, and now today's shoot. It wasn't just the situations surrounding the job that were the problem; it was the job itself.

I'd managed to convince myself that I could separate the two, but the truth was, one couldn't exist apart from the other. The work and the activities surrounding it were inextricably linked. By taking on the persona of an Angel, I had unwittingly signed a deal with the devil. And in doing so, I pretty much had surrendered every moral conviction I had.

No wonder Mike was so upset. I winced. *I entered that competition less than three months after we got married, and I have basically been disrespecting him—and God—ever since. Why didn't he say anything?* Then I realized he had. Mike made his feelings perfectly clear when he excused himself from the after-party, when he walked out of the photographer's apartment in Brooklyn, and when he shared his frustrations with me over having other men gawk at my photos. I just hadn't been listening.

I couldn't get away from that shoot quickly enough. After almost twelve months of ignoring every hint, intuition, and prick of conscience, the light had finally clicked on. And there was only one person I wanted to see.

As soon as Mike walked in the door that evening, I clung to him like there was no tomorrow.

"I am so sorry," I told him. "I never meant to hurt you. I promise."

As Mike held me and I shared my dawning realization with him, I could practically feel the relief pulsing through his arms.

"Thank God, baby." He gently rocked me back and forth. "I've been praying so hard for you. I knew God would open your eyes to the truth. I just knew it."

⟨∞⟩

I devoted the next several weeks to digging into the Bible and spending time in fervent prayer. I knew that God loved me unconditionally and that He had forgiven me the moment I expressed true repentance for my sins. But for the life of me, I couldn't understand why He would allow me to win the Victoria's Secret competition if everything it entailed was wrong.

God, I prayed, *I really need Your guidance. I know that You can bring all things together for good. And You never would have allowed me to win that competition if You didn't intend to bring something redemptive out of it somehow. Yet virtually everything that has happened since then has stood in direct opposition to what You want for my life. I don't know what to do, Lord. I desperately want to be a strong, faithful Christian and an honorable wife. Help me to understand what Your plan is. Help me to understand what You want me to do.*

Over the next several days I sought the counsel of a myriad of friends and family members, asking for their advice. Their responses ran the gamut from the predictable—"This is your dream. You've worked too hard to throw it all away now" and "Guys are always going to lust after you and other models. That's not your fault"—to the more godly: "You have to do what you think is right in the eyes of God" and "You and Mike need to seek God's leading on this together."

But not one person came right out and told me I should walk away from my newfound fame. Even Mike wouldn't tell me what I should do. Every time I asked him if he thought I should just quit altogether, he'd simply say, "I can't make this decision for you, Ky. All I can do is pray for you and love you unconditionally either way."

Still searching for answers, I turned to the Bible for wisdom. That's when I stumbled across 1 John 2:15-17: "Do not love the world or anything in the world. If anyone loves the world, love for the Father is not in them. For everything in the world—the lust of the flesh, the lust of the eyes, and the pride of life—comes not from the Father but from the world. The world and its desires pass away, but whoever does the will of God lives forever."

There was no question. The Bible was perfectly clear. I couldn't love the world and love God. I couldn't speak for anyone else, but I knew I couldn't continue to pursue a career as a supermodel—let alone a Victoria's Secret model—and still live a life that was honoring to God. The desires for personal fame and glory would always stand in direct opposition to the kind of humility and modesty God desired. And they would forever stand in the way of my becoming the kind of God-honoring wife Mike deserved—the kind of woman I read about in Proverbs 31:

Who can find a virtuous and capable wife?
    She is more precious than rubies.
Her husband can trust her,
    and she will greatly enrich his life.
She brings him good, not harm,
    all the days of her life. . . .

She is clothed with strength and dignity,
    and she laughs without fear of the future.
When she speaks, her words are wise,
    and she gives instructions with kindness. . . .

Her children stand and bless her.
    Her husband praises her:
"There are many virtuous and capable women
        in the world,
    but you surpass them all!"

Charm is deceptive, and beauty does not last;
  but a woman who fears the LORD will be greatly praised.
Reward her for all she has done.
  Let her deeds publicly declare her praise.

PROVERBS 31:10-12, 25-26, 28-31, NLT

Those words jumped out at me like a billboard along a deserted highway. I had my answer. I knew what I had to do.

Chapter 25

TRUTH AND CONSEQUENCES

Anyone who belongs to Christ has become a new
person. The old life is gone; a new life has begun!

2 CORINTHIANS 5:17, NLT

"SERIOUSLY?" Mike asked, his eyes wide with hope.

"Seriously." I took his face in my hands and kissed him gently
on the lips. "No more Victoria's Secret. No more lingerie. No more
swimsuits. I'm done with all of it." My conviction was growing
with each word.

Mike was so overwhelmed he couldn't speak. He simply kissed
me and wrapped me in his arms. Finally he managed a whisper:
"Thank You, Lord."

We stood there for a moment, basking in how much we had to
be thankful for—Mike, that the Lord had finally opened my eyes
to the devastating impact my career was having on both our marriage and my walk with the Lord; and me, that I had a husband
who was strong enough in his faith to sustain both of us while I
struggled to find my way out of the darkness.

234 || I'M NO ANGEL

Sure, Mike could have demanded that I quit my job months ago. But he knew it wasn't so much a question of changing my career as it was of changing my heart—and that's not something you can force. A genuine heart change usually evolves over time, like a caterpillar emerging from a cocoon. Mike simply remained faithful in prayer and waited patiently for the Lord to complete His work in me. And for that, I will be forever grateful—to both of them.

Announcing my decision to Mike was one thing. Facing my agency, employers, and everyone in the Victoria's Secret brand, I feared, would be another. But amazingly, the Lord proved faithful, and walking away ended up being worlds easier than I could have ever imagined.

Though I had done several shoots, red-carpet events, and an autograph signing for Victoria's Secret since winning the competition, I hadn't officially signed a contract with them, so I was under no legal obligation to continue the relationship. Even so, I was sure things would blow up when they heard about my decision. After all, they'd invested considerable time and effort in me, and I was pretty sure they wouldn't understand why I'd even consider leaving after reaching the top. After all, this was what I'd spent most of my life pursuing—not to mention that I'd beaten out many girls to get there. For someone looking through the eyes of faith, this decision was a no-brainer. But for someone who didn't share my values, it must have seemed like insanity.

To my great surprise and relief, there was no conversation, no discussion, no fireworks. My agency handled everything on my behalf. I didn't even have to state my case or defend myself. The Lord worked out everything in His perfect way.

In spite of the challenges I faced along the way, I will always be grateful for the opportunity I was given by Victoria's Secret. The experience taught me so much about myself, and ultimately it opened my eyes to my true priorities. It also gave me the chance to share my faith with Katelyn and Tika, and that was worth more than all the fashion shows, private dressing rooms, and red-carpet events on earth.

As for IMG, I still had a few small print jobs remaining on my schedule that I needed to honor, but by God's grace, they all were completely benign—just showcasing shoes and handbags. Once those obligations had been met, we simply parted company.

As doors continued to close on my old life in New York, I settled into my new life in northern Montana. For a while I just concentrated on studying the Word and seeking the Lord's wisdom on how to become a stronger Christian and the most faithful wife I could be. God had begun an excellent work in me, and I was committed to continuing down that path.

As God transformed my heart, my outward appearance started changing to match. I had my hair extensions taken out, and I let my hair return to its original color. I stopped getting spray tans, said no to tanning beds, and ditched the false eyelashes and heavy makeup in favor of a more natural look. After years of obsessing over my appearance and my weight so I could gain the approval of agents, clients, and casting directors, I was finally able to drop the facade and just be myself again.

When we first met, Mike told me he appreciated the fact that I was a simple, old-fashioned country girl who loved the Lord. I had strayed from that as I grew more and more obsessed with becoming an Angel. *From now on,* I promised myself, *that is exactly what he's going to get.*

Days I'd once spent scouring the Internet for fan postings or media blurbs now were spent turning our Montana lake house into a home. And evenings that used to be wasted with forced mingling at champagne-drenched parties and red-carpet events now were replaced with cuddling on the couch with Mike watching movies and studying the Bible together or lying out on the dock staring up at the magnificent star-filled Montana sky.

We'd exchanged the seemingly endless cacophony of car horns, ambulance sirens, and construction crews for the melodious chirp of crickets and the rustling of leaves blowing in the breeze. The congested steel- and concrete-lined streets of Manhattan gave way to wide-open farmland, sparkling lakes, and beautiful snow-capped mountains. It was the perfect backdrop for a complete transformation of body, mind, and spirit.

As for Mike and me, we were falling in love with each other all over again. No longer separated by some two thousand miles, we were making up for lost time by spending every moment we could together—hunting, fishing, camping, going for long walks in the woods, and growing in our relationships with the Lord. After much searching, we were led to a wonderful church just outside Kalispell that we absolutely loved. Mike and I became good friends with the pastor and his wife, and we even started hosting weekend marriage retreats in our home.

Another unexpected blessing of this new season was that our house became a hub for family gatherings. After years of missing out on my little brother's baseball games and school activities because of my work and travel, I was finally able to spend some quality time with him. I was also able to connect with Mike's son, Noah. Not only was I getting to know him, but I was also falling head over heels for the little guy.

It's funny—I'd always thought being a Victoria's Secret Angel would be the most glamorous, exciting job in the world. But when it was all said and done, that title couldn't compare to being Mrs. Kylie Bisutti: wife, stepmom, and child of God.

⤜∽

Of course, all actions have consequences, and even though I'd embraced a Christ-centered future, the demons of my past continued to haunt me. Almost a year after I decided to walk away from modeling provocative clothing, the issue of *FHM* I was featured in hit the newsstands—and with it, the torrid images I'd wanted to put behind me forever. My values might have changed radically over the past seven months, but everything the world stood for remained the same. I could make godly decisions related to my future, but I couldn't control how others chose to exploit my past.

And thanks to the Internet, there will always be dozens of images of me out there I wish didn't exist. They stand as a sobering reminder of where I've been—but also as tangible proof of how far God has brought me since then. While those images may never go away, I can assure you that the girl in them no longer exists. As the Bible says in 2 Corinthians 5:17, "Anyone who belongs to Christ has become a new person. The old life is gone; a new life has begun!" (NLT). That statement has been poignantly true in my life. And while I wish I could snap my fingers and make those photographs go away, they have become an important part of my testimony—a powerful reminder of the consequences of sin and the depths of God's redemptive grace.

As confident as I was in my decision to quit, I quickly realized that didn't mean all other temptations would magically disappear. Shortly after turning in my wings, I received a call from *Sports Illustrated* asking if I'd be interested in auditioning for their famous swimsuit edition. Despite all that God had been teaching me over the past several months, for the briefest of moments, I was tempted. *Well,* I rationalized, *maybe if I stick with a sporty one-piece that doesn't reveal too much, it would be okay.*

That's precisely how the enemy works. He's aware of our weaknesses, and he's always trying to deceive us into justifying behaviors and decisions we know are wrong. I'd fallen for this lie before, but I wasn't falling for it again. The Lord had opened my eyes to the way men view the women in those magazines, and I had no intention of dishonoring God or my husband or starting down that slippery slope again. The enemy is strong, but thankfully God is even stronger. And He is constantly working in me—molding me and shaping my desires.

In light of the nonstop media attention I'd received following the competition, it was fascinating to discover how quickly and completely I receded into the background of the modeling world. How could I be made to feel utterly indispensable one minute, only to be cast aside and forgotten the next? It was a good reminder of how fleeting fame is—just as God says in His Word.

By the time November rolled around and the ads for the next Victoria's Secret Fashion Show started to appear, the media had already moved on to the next big thing, and people were Googling another model's name. But for the first time in years, I could not have cared less. I'd seen the view from the mountaintop—everything fame and fortune had to offer—and I didn't want any part of it. I had moved on, and I had never been happier or more at peace in my life.

My heart still broke, though, for all the girls and young women out there who were filling the Twittersphere with words of anxiety and insecurity in anticipation of watching the Angels walk down the runway in a few weeks.

Those poor things, I thought as I read one angst-filled comment after another. *If only they knew what I know.*

Then it hit me like a lightning bolt—the answer to the question I'd been asking the Lord for months.

So that's why You let me win!

A smile teased at the corners of my mouth as I logged into my Twitter account for the first time in a long while and typed:

I quit being a VS model to become a Proverbs 31 wife.

My new life had begun.

Chapter 26

THE ULTIMATE WALK

"I know the plans I have for you," declares the LORD,
"plans to prosper you and not to harm you,
plans to give you hope and a future."

JEREMIAH 29:11

ALL MY LIFE, people have told me, "You have one of the best walks I've ever seen." But the truth is, my best walk didn't even get started until I gave up modeling.

When I won the Victoria's Secret Angel competition in 2009, I thought it was because God wanted me to fulfill my dream of becoming a world-famous fashion model. But now I know God wasn't looking to fulfill *my* dream. Nor was He interested in turning me into a famous model. As is usually the case, God's plans were infinitely larger, nobler, and more important than mine.

I finally discovered that God's desire wasn't for me to spend my life chasing after and promoting the world's definition of beauty as a supermodel. His plan was to transform me into a role model so I could dedicate my life to pursuing *His* definition of beauty.

But before I could help others understand what true beauty was, I had to learn that lesson myself.

When I first started out in modeling, I was no different from the thousands of girls tweeting on the night of the Fashion Show about needing to lose weight or bemoaning their imperfect complexions or wishing they were more beautiful. Like them, I thought the women walking the runway and gracing the pages of the Victoria's Secret catalog were absolutely perfect. And I, too, had been obsessed with chasing that kind of perfection.

It never occurred to me that parading down a runway in nothing but a bra and panties while millions of men ogled and applauded was inappropriate and even immodest. To me, it just looked sexy and glamorous and exciting. Now, however, I know better.

There is nothing glamorous about being treated like a piece of meat. And there is no such thing as perfection this side of heaven. Even the Angels themselves aren't perfect. Physically beautiful? Yes. But perfect? No. The resplendently flowing hair, the impeccable tans, the flawless skin, the pencil-thin waists, the voluptuous curves—it's mostly an illusion achieved through the wisp of an airbrush or the click of a mouse. And God in His infinite wisdom allowed me to see and experience that world firsthand.

God also opened my eyes to some of the horrific elements that often go hand in hand with the industry: the sex trafficking, the extreme surgeries, the drug abuse, the verbal abuse, the eating disorders, the infidelity, the lies, the deception, the betrayal, the pornography. Early in my career, I thought that the higher I climbed in modeling, the better things would get—that it was just a matter of paying my dues before the big payoff at the top. But the higher I climbed, the worse things got. The pressure, the loneliness, the deception, the ridiculous expectations—none of it changed; it just intensified. Skin shots became "art"; seedy guys trying to lure models into the back of an SUV became arrogant celebrities trolling for a hookup; and pot-smoking roommates became champagne-swilling supermodels. The same immoral or disreputable things I'd felt pressured to do to make it to the top suddenly were the things I was expected to do if I wanted to stay at the top.

Nothing got better. And nothing changed—except, of course, *me.*

I believe God allowed me to walk through the fire and see the best and the worst the industry had to offer so I could come out on the other side stronger and wiser, with my eyes fully opened to the truth. And now I believe He is calling me to share what I've learned, with the hope that other people won't have to learn the hard way, as I did.

After getting a glimpse behind the curtain into the world's definition of beauty, I know with certainty that true beauty isn't measured in pounds and inches. And it's not something that can be airbrushed over or added in with Photoshop. True beauty comes from within. Ultimately, it's a reflection of God's love in us.

The Bible tells us that "the LORD does not look at the things people look at. People look at the outward appearance, but the LORD looks at the heart" (1 Samuel 16:7). In other words, beauty in God's eyes is determined by our inner qualities, by our capacity to love and be loved. God doesn't care what we look like; He only cares that we love Him wholly and unconditionally and that we love one another, as well.

During my years in the industry, I encountered many physically beautiful women, but some of them were so lacking in character, kindness, and compassion that it was hard to think of them as anything but cold and harsh. Likewise, some of the most beautiful people I've met haven't been attractive by society's standards. But their kindness and genuineness give them an inner beauty that outshines any swimsuit model.

This lesson about the importance of inner beauty took me long enough to grasp, but God was patient, and eventually He broke through to me, due to His Word and the tangible example of Mike's love. I could walk into a room as pale as a sheet, my hair in tangles, my lips chapped, circles under my eyes, and a colossal zit smack-dab in the middle of my face, and Mike would still tell me I'm beautiful. He doesn't see me as the world sees me; he sees me the way God sees me. And God sees every one of us as beautiful. We are, after all, made in His image. We make ourselves ugly by turning away from Him and getting entangled in things He despises, like pride, greed, and lust. But the more we cling to virtues like humility, selflessness, modesty, and purity, the more beautiful we become—not only in His eyes, but also in the eyes of others. You can't airbrush that.

People often ask me if I regret giving up everything I forfeited when I turned my back on my modeling career—the money, the fame, the parties, the legions of admirers. I always tell them that what I gave up pales in comparison to the sacrifice Jesus made for me on the cross. Christ didn't die so I could travel the world in style, drive a fancy car, and live in a palatial estate. He died so that someday I could sit at the feet of my Father for all eternity. And there's not a modeling contract in the world that could match that.

God had something much bigger and better in mind for me than being a Victoria's Secret model, and He orchestrated it more seamlessly than any agent or casting director ever could have. Not only did He direct every step of my journey, but He also ensured that when the time was right, my words would have validity and I would have a platform from which to share them.

That's why I believe God allowed me to win that competition. Had I lost—or if I hadn't made it as far as I did—my message would have been written off as sour grapes. *Of course she's railing against the industry,* some people would say. *She didn't make it.* But I did make it. I walked the most prestigious runway in the world, and I held one of the most coveted titles in modeling.

When I first walked away from modeling, my intent wasn't to stop modeling altogether—I just didn't want to do lingerie, swimsuits, and other clothing that would be categorized as immodest. But as I continued to grow in my relationship with the Lord, I started to lose the desire to model at all. Regardless of the type of clothing, I knew that modeling promotes the world's sense of beauty. This wasn't the type of beauty I wanted to endorse for girls and women. Not only that, but the temptation would always be there to be thinner, prettier, and more in demand. I'd seen how addictive those desires can become, and I didn't want any part of it anymore.

And now God has given me a nobler calling—teaching girls and young women about the importance of dressing and behaving modestly, helping them understand that true beauty comes from within, and encouraging them in their walk with the Lord. It's a ministry I've unknowingly spent my whole life preparing for, and it feels like one of the ways God is redeeming the ugly parts of my past and turning them into something beautiful.

My Christian walk hasn't always been easy, and there are still days I have to battle the temptation to obsess over the number on the scale or to pick up an outfit that shows a little too much skin.

But we were never given a guarantee that it would be easy. We all struggle from time to time, and we all make mistakes. But sometimes God uses those mistakes as an opportunity for us to learn and grow. My whole journey is evidence of that.

Something I learned early on is that there's a big difference between accepting Christ into your heart and walking with Him on a daily basis. Both require a leap of faith through grace alone. But actively living out your faith also requires conviction, discipline, and a commitment to stand in direct opposition to what the world says is good. It's not always easy. But then again, nothing worthwhile ever is.

A lot has been said about me since I made the decision to quit my career in modeling—some good, some bad. I have to agree on one point, though—I *do* have a great walk.

And it's even better now that I've let go of my wings.

THE MASTER'S MAKEOVER

30 Days to a More Beautiful You

Your beauty should not come from outward adornment,
such as elaborate hairstyles and the wearing of gold jewelry
or fine clothes. Rather, it should be that of your inner self,
the unfading beauty of a gentle and quiet spirit,
which is of great worth in God's sight.

1 PETER 3:3-4

DESPITE WHAT THE modeling world might lead us to believe, true beauty has nothing to do with outward appearances. The more we focus on what we look like on the outside, the more insecure we become. The world has an impossibly narrow definition of beauty, and by those standards, we'll never be thin enough, pretty enough, or good enough.

But fortunately, that's not how God measures our worth. We have value simply because we are His children. The more we focus on getting our hearts right with the Lord and honoring Him, the more secure and confident we will become—and the more we will exude true beauty. After all, outer beauty will fade away, but the godly qualities we possess will grow and become more beautiful over time!

Instead of focusing on superficial beauty, I encourage you to spend the next thirty days focusing on an inner beauty makeover. I pray that this devotional will help transform your heart, your body, your mind, and your soul and put you on the path to becoming a happier, healthier, more beautiful you.

God bless,
Kylie

RENEWING YOUR HEART

Day 1

MADE IN GOD'S IMAGE

God created mankind in his own image,
in the image of God he created them;
male and female he created them.

GENESIS 1:27

THROUGH MY YEARS in the modeling industry, I learned a hard truth: your perceived worth is based on characteristics you can't control. If you have genes that predisposed you to be five feet ten and 110 pounds with long, thin legs, you're considered worthwhile. If your genes made you five feet two and muscular, you might be an ideal soccer player and a fantastic human being—but in the modeling world, you're worth nothing.

Fortunately, appearance is not the way *true* worth is measured. The Bible makes it clear that we have inherent value because we are made in God's image. As humans, we are His most precious creation, and He made us like Him in special ways. He gave us minds that can seek to know Him and hearts that can love Him. He gave us creativity, compassion, and understanding. He gave us an important role in this world, and He wants to have a relationship with us.

We have worth. God Himself loves and values us. There's nothing we can achieve or become in this life that will make God think we are more worthwhile than He does already. And if God thinks we have great value, who are we to argue with Him?

What traits do you think give someone value?

How might believing you are made in God's image change your sense of worth?

True beauty tip: *You are worthwhile to God.*

Day 2
WHO AM I?

God decided in advance to adopt us into his own family
by bringing us to himself through Jesus Christ. This is
what he wanted to do, and it gave him great pleasure.

EPHESIANS 1:5, NLT

THE WORLD ENCOURAGES us to define ourselves based on any number of external factors: what we look like, what other people think of us, how much money we earn, what kind of career we have. But God says that none of those things matter—none of those things can define who we really are.

Throughout my life I've filled various roles: daughter, sister, wife, step-mom, model, Victoria's Secret Runway Angel. Some of those roles have shaped me in positive ways; others have had a harmful effect on me. It's tempting to let my identity become wrapped up in those titles or positions—to start to think that they make me who I am. But no matter how good the roles are—even when they're blessings from the Lord—they can't determine my true identity.

God says that our identity can come only from our position as His children. We have inherent value because He adopted us and brought us into His family. Even when all our other roles are stripped away, that's something no one can take from us. God always will be our Father, and we always will be His daughters.

What roles do you tend to let define you?

What does it mean to you that God has adopted you into His family?

True beauty tip: You have inherent value as God's child.

Day 3

FINDING YOUR WORTH

You are a people holy to the LORD your God.
Out of all the peoples on the face of the earth, the
LORD has chosen you to be his treasured possession.

DEUTERONOMY 14:2

ALL OF US SOMETIMES doubt our value because we don't measure up to the world's standards in some way. We let other people tell us we're not pretty enough, thin enough, smart enough, talented enough, or likable enough.

Whether we're trying out for a sports team, auditioning for a play, or applying for a job, it's easy to let our sense of worth rise or fall on the outcome. When I was cast in shows during Fashion Week, I felt good about myself. When I wasn't what a client was looking for, I felt inadequate. But the truth is, we're the same whether the person on the other end of the phone says yes or no. We don't have to give others the power to determine our worth.

Our value has nothing to do with what we wear, how we look, how many friends we have, or how successful we become. We are daughters of the King, and we have great value because God says we do! As believers, we are God's special treasures. He loves us so much that He sent Jesus to die so we could be with Him forever. When other people question your worth because you don't fit their ideals, remember that God gave up everything to bring you new life.

Where are you looking to find your worth?

What do you think it means to be God's "treasured possession"?

True beauty tip: You are a daughter of the King.

Day 4
PEOPLE PLEASING

Our purpose is to please God, not people.
He alone examines the motives of our hearts.

1 THESSALONIANS 2:4, NLT

IT'S A NATURAL HUMAN DESIRE to want to be liked, accepted, and appreciated. But if we're not careful, that longing can get out of whack and pretty much take over our lives, influencing us to do things we'd never do otherwise.

That's exactly what happened to me. When I was young, I loved being Daddy's little girl. But as I got older and Dad and I drifted apart, I found myself desperate for attention—especially male attention. By the time I was in junior high, I was posting pictures of myself on Myspace, hoping to get a bazillion comments, and by the time I was in high school, I was dressing provocatively, wanting the boys to notice me.

Unfortunately, that people-pleasing tendency didn't stop in adulthood. When I became a model, I wanted to be accepted, to have people think not only that I was beautiful, but also that I was sweet and nice and easy to get along with. And along the way, I ended up making compromises—doing photo shoots and taking jobs I never would have if I weren't trying so hard to make other people happy.

The Bible says that our purpose should be to please God, not people. He knows our hearts, and He knows who we're ultimately trying to honor—ourselves, the men in our lives, our employers, or Him. We will never be the women God wants us to be if our hearts are continually chasing after human approval.

Take an honest look at your heart. Who are you seeking to please?

What is one thing you need to say no to this week out of a desire to honor God, not people?

True beauty tip: *Live to please God, not people.*

Day 5
RESTING IN GOD'S LOVE

> I am convinced that neither death nor life, neither angels
> nor demons, neither the present nor the future, nor any
> powers, neither height nor depth, nor anything else
> in all creation, will be able to separate us from the love
> of God that is in Christ Jesus our Lord.
>
> ROMANS 8:38-39

WHEN I ATTENDED a Christian camp one summer in high school, I felt so drawn to God. I wanted to experience His love and forgiveness, but I was scared. I had blown it that year by lying to my parents and losing my virginity in a bad relationship. What if God couldn't forgive me for the wrong things I had done? What if He didn't want me as a follower because I just wasn't good enough?

It was a youth leader who first showed me unconditional love and gave me the courage to believe that God could love me too. She encouraged me to confess everything to Him and receive His forgiveness. I did, and my life was changed because of it.

It's powerful to realize that Someone knows everything about us—our mistakes and our successes, our best moments and our absolute worst—and still loves us completely, without reservation. How amazing is that? The Bible tells us that nothing can separate us from God. Nothing! Not our mistakes. Not our appearance or personality. Not those things about ourselves we feel insecure about. Not even our sin, if we've confessed it to Him. He loves us because we are His.

What is holding you back from trusting in God's unconditional love?

How could accepting God's love free you from your fears?

True beauty tip: *God loves you unconditionally.*

Day 6
TRUE SECURITY

This is how God showed his love among us:
He sent his one and only Son into the
world that we might live through him.

1 JOHN 4:9

IT'S AMAZING HOW much energy we can expend by competing with others. We think if we can prove we're the best, we'll feel secure finally. During my years of modeling, I made a few friends. But more often, a sense of competition overshadowed the interactions between models. Girls were so busy comparing themselves to each other and trying to come out on top that there was no room for camaraderie. Unfortunately, success was so short lived that no one really found the security they were seeking.

The thing is, true security doesn't have anything to do with our own talents or accomplishments. It has to do with knowing who we are in God's eyes.

When we rest in God's love, we're reminded that He is enough for us. When we let our hearts be filled with His love, we can finally relax. We're secure—free from the need to prove anything. Instead, we can put our energy toward becoming the kind of women God created us to be. And that's truly beautiful.

Where are you trying to find your security?

What is one thing you could do this week to rest more fully in God's love?

True beauty tip: You are secure in God's love.

RENEWING YOUR BODY

Day 7

DISCOVERING INNER BEAUTY

Your beauty should not come from outward adornment,
such as elaborate hairstyles and the wearing of gold jewelry
or fine clothes. Rather, it should be that of your inner self,
the unfading beauty of a gentle and quiet spirit,
which is of great worth in God's sight.

1 PETER 3:3-4

THESE VERSES FROM 1 Peter are so freeing. We're reminded not to make our external appearance our primary concern. Why? Because when we do, we're focusing on something that will fade and neglecting something that will last.

I know firsthand how many hours are spent fixing hair and makeup before a photo shoot—all to capture one fleeting second where everything looks perfect. The truth is, almost everything about our appearance is temporary. The clothes we buy today will be out of style next year. The highlights we pay to put in our hair will need to be redone next month. Our bodies and faces will change as we get older.

What *will* last is our inner character. When Peter writes of the "unfading beauty of a gentle and quiet spirit," I think he means that a woman who loves the Lord and seeks to honor Him will *always* seem beautiful. Others will be drawn to her because of her gentleness, compassion, mercy, and wisdom, and those qualities will increase as she ages. That's the kind of beauty I want.

How is focusing too much on your external appearance distracting you from developing inner beauty?

How do you define true inner beauty?

True beauty tip: *Genuine beauty comes from inside.*

Day 8
YOUR BODY AS A TEMPLE

Do you not know that your bodies are temples of the
Holy Spirit, who is in you, whom you have received
from God? You are not your own; you were bought
at a price. Therefore honor God with your bodies.

1 CORINTHIANS 6:19-20

IN OUR CULTURE, we're so focused on individual rights that this idea of
belonging to God, rather than ourselves, seems strange. After all, I've seen
what happens when clients view a model as their property. They might chop
off her hair or dye it without asking, make her squeeze into clothes that are
too small, and have her pose in whatever way fits the image they're after.
I've had my fill of giving up the rights to my body to people who don't have
my best interests at heart.

But that's exactly the point: God *does* have our best interests at heart.
He didn't buy us with the high price of Jesus' blood so we would become
His property. He did it so we would be free forever from the chains of sin
and death.

What's even more amazing is that God chooses to send His Spirit to
live within believers. That should change everything about the way we view
ourselves. We are His, and we need to honor God with our bodies. After all,
they are His dwelling place!

How do you react to the idea that you belong to God?

Which actions or attitudes in your life right now are most honoring to
God? Which are least honoring?

True beauty tip: *Your body is a temple of the Holy Spirit.*

Day 9
HONORING GOD WITH YOUR BODY

> I urge you, brothers and sisters, in view of God's mercy,
> to offer your bodies as a living sacrifice, holy and
> pleasing to God—this is your true and proper worship.
>
> ROMANS 12:1

WHAT DOES IT MEAN to let our bodies be living sacrifices to God? I think it's tied in with the idea we talked about yesterday—that our bodies are dwelling places of the Holy Spirit. We are His, so we need to honor Him with our bodies.

My decision to quit being a lingerie model had to do with choosing to honor the Lord with my body. Modeling sexy lingerie was something that brought me attention, but I realized it was encouraging people to look at me in a way that wasn't godly. Plus, I was taking something God intended to be sacred between a husband and a wife and making it public.

Even if we're not on the runway, we all have a tendency to dishonor our bodies. Some of us have starved ourselves in an attempt to get thinner and reach a worldly ideal of beauty. Some of us have cut ourselves or used harmful substances or given our bodies away cheaply in an effort to get someone's attention. But we are worth more than that! God has given us our bodies, and His Holy Spirit lives within them. They are good, they are beautiful, and they are His. They are to be used to bring God glory.

What things in your life do you need to change to more consistently honor God with your body?

What does it mean to let your body be a living sacrifice to God?

True beauty tip: God created your body, and it brings Him glory when you honor Him with it.

Day 10
EMBRACING GOD'S CREATIVITY

> O Lord, what a variety of things you have made!
>   In wisdom you have made them all.
>   The earth is full of your creatures. . . .
> May the glory of the Lord continue forever!
>   The Lord takes pleasure in all he has made!
>
> PSALM 104:24, 31, NLT

I'VE ALWAYS BEEN an outdoor girl. I love being out in nature, and I'm amazed at the incredible variety in God's creation. He could have kept it simple when He created the universe, but instead He came up with a mind-boggling array of plant and animal life.

The Lord took that same creativity and applied it to people, too. With more than seven billion people alive today, no two have the same fingerprints. (Not even identical twins!) No two have exactly the same personality, attitudes, or gifts. So with all that God-given variety in the world, why do we expect we all should fit into the same mold when it comes to our appearance?

Psalm 139 says that God knit each of us together in our mother's womb. He made us the way we are on purpose—and He takes pleasure in all He has made. He sees us as beautiful, and He is working in our lives to make us even more beautiful in His eyes. That has nothing to do with our measurements or our wardrobes and everything to do with the way we are becoming more and more like Christ.

As we become conformed to His image, we begin to show more evidence of the fruit of the Spirit—things like joy, peace, and patience. We begin to respond to others with the love of Christ. And that's beautiful.

In what ways do you sometimes wish you fit the "ideal" mold?

How can you celebrate the unique way God created you?

True beauty tip: *God made you uniquely beautiful.*

Day 11

SEARCHING FOR AUTHENTICITY

You have searched me, LORD,
and you know me.
You know when I sit and when I rise;
you perceive my thoughts from afar.

PSALM 139:1-2

HAVE YOU EVER SEEN an ad where the model looked incredible and thought, *That can't be real?* Most likely, it wasn't. Photoshop is the modeling industry's best friend. It's not enough that models starve themselves, wear tons of makeup, and sometimes even resort to surgery to fit some crazy ideal of beauty. On top of all that, some computer program is probably making their thighs thinner, their necks longer, their lips plumper, their skin smoother. Then others see that image and try to live up to an ideal that isn't even real.

So much of what the world says is beautiful is just fake. But as Christians, we're called to be people of truth. I don't want to get caught up in presenting an image that's false. After all, the Bible reminds us that God knows each one of us inside and out. He not only knows what we look like without makeup, He knows who we are deep inside—our thoughts, our feelings, our insecurities, our imperfections. We don't have to hide from Him. He sees us fully, and He loves us completely.

Instead of getting stuck trying to be someone we're not, we need to celebrate the women we are—the authentic, real women God has created us to be.

In what ways do false ideas of beauty affect you?

How could you be more authentic in the way you look or in the ways you interact with others?

True beauty tip: *God knows and loves the real you.*

Day 12
VALUING MODESTY

I also want the women to dress modestly, with decency
and propriety, adorning themselves, not with elaborate
hairstyles or gold or pearls or expensive clothes.

1 TIMOTHY 2:9

WHEN I WAS A TEEN, I thought modesty meant wearing long, shapeless dresses or other hopelessly old-fashioned clothes. Who would want to look that unappealing? I wanted to look good, and I wanted others to notice me. That was my attitude until God convicted me and I started rethinking the whole idea of modesty.

Modesty is partly about the clothes we wear, but it's also an attitude. I'm learning that being modest means not dressing to get attention. It also means not using sex appeal to make men notice me. I've done photo shoots where I was fully clothed but still immodest—because the purpose was to use sex to sell a product.

The apostle Paul lays it on the line when he tells women not to seek attention from what they wear, but instead to let their service to God be what sets them apart and makes them appealing. When we dress provocatively, we're devaluing ourselves because we're encouraging others to ignore everything about us except our external appearance. I want my clothes to reflect my true value as a woman—someone who is trying to be beautiful both inside and out.

Think honestly about the way you dress. What are you encouraging others to focus on when they look at you?

What can you do this week to make your outward appearance reflect your inner value?

True beauty tip: *Develop an attitude of modesty.*

RENEWING YOUR MIND

Day 13
THE WORLD'S LIES

Do not love the world or anything in the world. If anyone
loves the world, love for the Father is not in them.
For everything in the world—the lust of the flesh,
the lust of the eyes, and the pride of life—
comes not from the Father but from the world.

1 JOHN 2:15-16

LIFE HASN'T CHANGED that much since those words were written some two thousand years ago. Back then the world was focused on physical pleasure, materialism, and personal success—and it still is today. The details may be different, but we still face the challenge of combating the lies our culture feeds us and the cravings it builds in us.

Many of us find ourselves craving the material things this world can offer. When I was first married, I had left New York and was content to put an end to my modeling career. But the moment my mother-in-law showed me the entry form for the Victoria's Secret contest, all of my cravings for fame and attention returned in full force. I was so focused on the here and now that my love for God started to get crowded out.

When we keep God at the forefront of our minds, we'll be protected from many of the lies our culture tries to feed us. We'll remember that He is what is most important in life. Our relationship with Him—not fame or pleasure or attention—is what will last.

What cravings do you have for worldly things?

How would a focus on eternal things change your priorities?

True beauty tip: Only what God offers us will last.

Day 14
THE RIGHT STANDARDS

See to it that no one takes you captive through
hollow and deceptive philosophy, which depends
on human tradition and the elemental spiritual
forces of this world rather than on Christ.

COLOSSIANS 2:8

WHEN I LOOK BACK on my modeling career, I can't believe it took me so long to realize that some of my jobs were inappropriate. But the truth is, I fell victim to the "hollow and deceptive philosophy" that Paul talks about in Colossians. I convinced myself that doing a topless shoot was okay if nothing showed. I bought the lie that since men might look at me lustfully even when I was fully clothed, it didn't matter if I posed provocatively. I was blinded by human thinking.

It's easy for us to get caught up in the world's way of looking at life. If we're not careful, we'll suddenly find ourselves agreeing with a lot of things that are clearly contrary to God's Word. We'll live as if today is all that matters and as if accumulating things is the point of our existence. We might even think that God's primary purpose is to bring us material success and happiness. We'll lose our way and move farther and farther from God's redemptive truth.

We need to evaluate our attitudes in light of Scripture. Our perspective needs to be aligned with Christ's so we can become more and more like Him. He is the standard—our real model.

In what areas have you compromised your standards to look like the world's?

In what ways do you need to be intentional about imitating Christ?

True beauty tip: *Let Christ be your standard.*

Day 15
GOOD ENOUGH

God demonstrates his own love for us in this:
While we were still sinners, Christ died for us.

ROMANS 5:8

HAVE YOU EVER FELT like you weren't quite good enough just as you are? Maybe someone told you that you would look so good—if only you would lose ten pounds or dye your hair. Maybe someone told you that you would succeed—if only you would work harder or practice more. I'll never forget when my young cousin watched me get ready and said, "I think I want to stop eating so I can look like you." At age eight she had already internalized the message that she could be beautiful *if only* she changed something about herself.

If only hammers home the point that the only way we'll be okay is if we change. It tells us that the way we are now is not good enough.

The amazing truth is that God doesn't expect us to be good enough. He doesn't ask us to clean ourselves up before we come to Him; He sent Jesus to die even when we were still stuck in our sin. He knows we aren't good enough, but in His mercy He makes us *more* than good enough. In fact, He makes us holy in His sight!

If you have asked His forgiveness, you can stop trying so hard to measure up. All you need to do is rest in His lavish, unwavering love.

In what situations do you feel you don't measure up?

How might your perspective change knowing that God makes you "good enough"?

True beauty tip: *God's forgiveness makes you "good enough"!*

Day 16

TRANSFORMING YOUR MIND

> Do not conform to the pattern of this world,
> but be transformed by the renewing of your mind.
> Then you will be able to test and approve what
> God's will is—his good, pleasing and perfect will.
>
> ROMANS 12:2

I'LL NEVER FORGET when my agent told me she didn't want to see me again until I'd lost weight. Devastated, I went home and stared at myself in the mirror, convinced I was fat. But it was a lie. I was ignoring what I knew to be true and buying into the world's view of beauty. I was being conformed.

We have to discover the difference between being *con*formed and being *trans*formed. When we're being conformed to the world, we become just like it. We stop trusting our own judgment. We don't even believe our own eyes when we look in the mirror! We measure our bodies, our perspectives, even our opinions against the way we're "supposed" to look or think. We lose our individuality.

God has created us not to be clones, but to be unique individuals. He wants to change the way we think so we'll stop worrying about fitting in. He wants to lead us to something better—His will for our lives, which is good and pleasing and perfect. He has our best interests at heart. Through His grace, He will transform us into new people—the women He created us to be.

In what ways have you allowed yourself to be conformed to the world's standards?

What are some ways you would benefit from being transformed by God?

True beauty tip: Be transformed, not conformed.

Day 17

DEFINED BY GOD

Just as you accepted Christ Jesus as your Lord,
you must continue to follow him. Let your roots
grow down into him, and let your lives be built on him.
Then your faith will grow strong in the truth you were
taught, and you will overflow with thankfulness.

COLOSSIANS 2:6-7, NLT

IN OUR TECHNOLOGY-SATURATED ERA, we can be connected with popular culture just about every waking moment. We can get updates of celebrity news, keep up with fashion magazines, and measure our own popularity based on the responses we get on social media. The messages we receive every day begin to define us, yet so few are focused on anything meaningful.

When I was living in New York, I found myself slipping away from my faith and losing my identity. I realize now that I was spending almost all of my time focused on my career and almost no time in God's Word. But I recognize now that the only way we can stay grounded in the midst of those media messages is to read and study the Bible.

When we surround ourselves with God's Word, we get to know His voice. We begin to learn what He wants for us and from us. And the more we know Him, the more effectively we're able to evaluate the other messages we receive. When we're grounded in God's Word, we won't be swayed by a magazine article telling us how we should think or look. Our roots will grow deep into Christ, our faith will be strong, and our lives will overflow with thankfulness.

What is defining you?

How can you become more grounded in God's Word?

True beauty tip: Let the roots of your life grow deep into Christ.

Day 18

THE UNCHANGING ONE

"I am the Alpha and the Omega—the beginning and the
end," says the Lord God. "I am the one who is, who always
was, and who is still to come—the Almighty One."

REVELATION 1:8, NLT

WE'RE ALL LOOKING FOR SECURITY. In the midst of our crazy, fast-paced
culture, we want something we can count on, something that will stay the
same. But the sad truth is that at some point or another, people will fail us.

As I moved into my teen years, I longed for the closeness I'd once had
with my dad, but with his heavy work schedule and other stresses, he and I
gradually drifted apart. When I dated Jake, I wanted so badly to trust him
and to believe he'd be there for me no matter what—but he let me down.
Until I discovered Christ, I didn't know where to find the kind of security
I needed.

Jesus is the only One who will stick by us no matter what. Everyone
else will change, but God never will! The Bible tells us that He has always
existed and He always will. He is the beginning and the end. Nothing can
change Him, and nothing can change His love for us. He is our rock, the
unchanging, almighty God.

Who or what are you counting on for your security?

What comforts you about knowing God never changes?

True beauty tip: You can depend on God, who never changes.

RENEWING YOUR SOUL

Day 19

PUTTING GOD FIRST

Those who live according to the flesh have their minds
set on what the flesh desires; but those who live in
accordance with the Spirit have their minds set on what
the Spirit desires. The mind governed by the flesh is death,
but the mind governed by the Spirit is life and peace.

ROMANS 8:5-6

WHEN MOST PEOPLE hear the word *idolatry*, they assume it applies to people who worship man-made statues. But that's not the whole picture. The Bible says that anything that rules our lives is an idol. God is meant to have first place in our lives, so when we put anything else there, we're making an idol of it.

For much of my life, my desire to make it big in modeling was my idol. That directed almost every decision I made—like the choice to move to New York when I was sixteen or the decision to have a provocative photo taken so I could be represented by a top agency. My desire to be successful took over and moved me far from God. But when I let go of that desire, I found God's purpose for me. Once Jesus became my treasure, the rest of my life fell into place.

We can live by our fleshly desires and the idols that control our hearts, or we can live transformed lives, where Christ is our hearts' treasure. One way leads to a life that's shallow and ultimately unsatisfying. The better way leads to peace and a sense of purpose.

What things have become idols in your life?

What would it look like for you to turn those things over to God?

True beauty tip: *Make Jesus your heart's true treasure.*

Day 20
SERVING GOD

No one can serve two masters. Either you will
hate the one and love the other, or you will be
devoted to the one and despise the other.

MATTHEW 6:24

I'LL NEVER FORGET the day I realized I was going to have to quit my
dream job. My whole modeling career, I'd wanted to become a Victoria's
Secret model, and I'd finally made it. Yet I'd started to feel more and more
uncomfortable in that world. God was opening my eyes to the fact that I
couldn't glorify Him in my life while at the same time taking modeling jobs
that compromised His values. The disconnect was too great, and if I kept
trying to do both, I would end up despising one. I had to choose. Would I
serve the world, or would I serve God?

If we keep trying to serve two things, our consciences will bother us at
first. But the more we ignore them, the less sensitive they'll become. And
that's a dangerous path to start down. Eventually, if we keep choosing to
serve the world, we won't bring any glory to God in the way we're living.

It's a tough choice to make, but we can ask God to help us. He will give
us the wisdom to make the right decision, and He will give us the courage
to act on it. In the end, it will be more than worth it to serve only Him.

In what ways are you trying to serve both God *and* the world?

What changes do you need to make that will help you be more focused
on serving God?

True beauty tip: *Serve God alone.*

Day 21

NO COMPROMISE

Joyful are people of integrity,
    who follow the instructions of the LORD.
Joyful are those who obey his laws
    and search for him with all their hearts.
They do not compromise with evil,
    and they walk only in his paths.

PSALM 119:1-3, NLT

THIS PSALM SAYS that people of integrity refuse to compromise with evil. Most of us believe that, but it doesn't change the fact that it can be so tempting to give in—even on things we strongly believe in.

Many times we compromise because we're so focused on the outcome we want. We lose the perspective to evaluate the steps it will take to get there. When I was in high school, I wanted love and attention so badly. My main goal was to remain Jake's girlfriend, and because I was so focused on that, I was driven to do things that were against my convictions. Ultimately, compromising only brought me pain and guilt.

It's only when we live a life of obedience to God—searching for Him and staying on His path—that we will find joy. Not because everything will automatically go our way, but because we will be living the way God intended. We'll be pursuing things that please Him, and that's the only way we'll find true satisfaction.

Which of your goals do you think are pleasing to God?

How can you develop more integrity in your life?

True beauty tip: *We can find joy in doing what's right.*

Day 22
RUNNING THE RACE

Since we are surrounded by such a great cloud of
witnesses, let us throw off everything that hinders and
the sin that so easily entangles. And let us run with
perseverance the race marked out for us, fixing our eyes
on Jesus, the pioneer and perfecter of faith. For the joy
set before him he endured the cross, scorning its shame,
and sat down at the right hand of the throne of God.

HEBREWS 12:1-2

IMAGINE YOU'RE RUNNING a long race and you're starting to get tired. When
you look down, you realize that you're carrying a five-pound weight in each
hand, and you have a heavy pack strapped on your back. A rope is wrapped
around your ankles, and it's making you trip. What would you do? You'd
immediately get rid of the stuff that's slowing you down, right?

That's a great image to remember when we feel God prompting us to give
up something that is pulling us away from Him. When we sense that God
might want us to let go of something that's precious to us—maybe a dream
that's getting in the way of our walk with Christ—our instinct is to hold on
even more tightly. But the truth is, if something is tripping us up in the race
of faith, it doesn't matter how much we want that thing. It's only holding us
back, pulling us farther away from Jesus. When we have the courage to throw
it aside and follow Him, just think how freely we'll be able to run.

What is one thing that's holding you back in your race of faith?

What's the first step you can take in letting go of that thing?

True beauty tip: *Throw aside your burdens and run the race
of faith.*

Day 23

ACCEPTING FORGIVENESS

He does not punish us for all our sins;
    he does not deal harshly with us, as we deserve.
For his unfailing love toward those who fear him
    is as great as the height of the heavens above the earth.
He has removed our sins as far from us
    as the east is from the west.

PSALM 103:10-12, NLT

IN THE MODELING WORLD, airbrushing is the gold standard. The model has a blemish? Fix it electronically. The model's thighs look too big? Thin them digitally. Problems get covered up. They're still there, but no one can see them.

That's the way a lot of us think about the things we've done wrong. The best the world can offer is a way to cover up our sins and pretend they don't exist. But all of us who have felt guilt over a sin we've committed know that approach just isn't enough. No matter how much we try to distract ourselves, no matter how hard we try to cover it up, we know the problem is still there. We can't get away from it.

If it weren't for God, we'd be stuck with our guilt forever. But His forgiveness offers so much more. He alone is capable of taking away our sin and guilt. This psalm says that God removes our sins from us—as far as the east is from the west. That's much better than airbrushing. Praise the Lord for His forgiveness!

What sin or bad decision in your life do you still feel guilty about?

What is holding you back from accepting God's forgiveness?

True beauty tip: *God's forgiveness removes your sins completely.*

Day 24

BECOMING THE WOMAN GOD WANTS YOU TO BE

We ask God to give you complete knowledge of his will and to give you spiritual wisdom and understanding. Then the way you live will always honor and please the Lord, and your lives will produce every kind of good fruit. All the while, you will grow as you learn to know God better and better.

COLOSSIANS 1:9-10, NLT

WHEN IT COMES to our walk with the Lord, it's tempting to do the bare minimum. We know we've got the most important thing covered—salvation—so we're sometimes content with a faith that doesn't really change the way we live. For years, I thought Christianity mostly meant that God wanted me to be happy. I didn't understand that true faith goes far deeper.

Jesus told His disciples that He had come to bring full, abundant life (see John 10:10). He wants to give us more than the bare minimum—more joy, more freedom, more purpose. That's what the apostle Paul is talking about in these verses from Colossians. His prayer isn't for fame or professional success, but for God's will and spiritual wisdom. Our prayer should be the same—that our lives would honor God and that we would grow to know Him more and more.

We need to let God keep working in us to make us the women He created us to be. As we do, we'll be filled with a peace and a sense of purpose we've never had before.

What do you think an abundant life looks like?

What choices can you make this week that will help you get to know God better?

True beauty tip: The only way to a satisfying life is to know God.

BECOMING A
PROVERBS 31 WOMAN

Day 25

BECOMING A WOMAN
OF CHARACTER

> We can rejoice, too, when we run into problems and
> trials, for we know that they help us develop endurance.
> And endurance develops strength of character, and
> character strengthens our confident hope of salvation.
> And this hope will not lead to disappointment.
>
> ROMANS 5:3-5, NLT

STRONG CHARACTER doesn't just happen automatically when we start following Christ. As Paul writes in Romans 5, often it's through our struggles that our character is strengthened. That's certainly been true for me. It was in the craziness of the Victoria's Secret competition that I was able to share my faith with others, and it was when I experienced the turmoil of the modeling world that I found the strength to take a stand for what was right.

As our character develops, we won't view every personal setback as a catastrophe. Instead, we'll be able to see our circumstances through the lens of hope, knowing that someday God will redeem this world and make all things new. That gives us the perspective we need to face every challenge.

As we grow into women of character, we start realizing that life isn't just about us. We become aware of the needs around us, and we learn to respond with compassion. And ultimately God will use our struggles to create stronger faith in us. That's true character.

As you look back over your life, what challenges have strengthened your character?

What would it look like to rejoice in the midst of a trial you're facing now?

True beauty tip: *Our character is strengthened through struggles.*

Day 26
WORKING FOR GOD'S KINGDOM

Now all glory to God, who is able, through his
mighty power at work within us, to accomplish
infinitely more than we might ask or think.

EPHESIANS 3:20, NLT

ONE OF THE MOST AMAZING things about living for Christ is that God allows us to work with Him to share His love with the world. It's only been in the last few years that I've realized God can use me, and I'm already amazed at the opportunities He has put in my path.

God took my circumstances as a Victoria's Secret Runway Angel, including the less-than-perfect decisions that led me there, and used them for His glory. Now He's allowing me to be a wife, a stepmom, and a role model for young women, and I love it. I always believed I was born to walk the runway, but to be honest, I've never felt more fulfilled.

God has given you the privilege of joining Him too. That will look different for each person, depending on your gifts and the needs around you. But no matter what your gifts—even if you think you don't have any—God can use you! He can accomplish more through you than you could ever imagine.

How do you think God might want to use you and your gifts?

How do you see God working in the world around you? How could you join in?

True beauty tip: *God is working through you.*

Day 27
LIVING WITH STRENGTH AND DIGNITY

She is clothed with strength and dignity;
she can laugh at the days to come.

PROVERBS 31:25

STRENGTH AND DIGNITY—those are two characteristics I want to define my life. A strong woman has courage. She is not swayed by what others think; she trusts God and makes decisions based on what is right. I've lacked that strength at many times in my life, and I've had to deal with the consequences of choices I made because I was too worried about pleasing people. Having a strong character means we let God—not our own fears or emotions—guide us.

A dignified woman knows what she's worth. She doesn't beg for attention or desperately seek others' approval. She knows she is loved by God, and she responds by serving God and others. That's the kind of dignity God will help us attain when we put Him first in our lives.

One of the encouraging parts of this verse is that the woman described in Proverbs 31 doesn't struggle to develop these characteristics on her own. God Himself *clothes* her with strength and dignity! He gives us what we need before we even ask. He will equip us to accomplish the tasks He puts in front of us.

Who are some women you know who fit this description of strength and dignity?

How is God developing strength and dignity in your life?

True beauty tip: *A strong woman trusts in God.*

Day 28
SETTING AN EXAMPLE

Don't let anyone look down on you because you
are young, but set an example for the believers in
speech, in conduct, in love, in faith and in purity.

1 TIMOTHY 4:12

SOMETIMES WE FEEL as if our individual choices don't matter, as if no
one notices what we do. But the truth is, others *are* watching us. When
I tweeted about quitting modeling, I was amazed by the comments I got
from teen girls who read my story and were challenged to think about how
they dressed or how to honor God with their bodies. It wasn't until I had
a change of heart that I realized how God might use me as a positive influence. Not because there's anything special about me, but simply because
Christ shines through me.

All of us have an opportunity to influence those around us—whether
they're our family members and friends, people in our communities, or
even random strangers who happen to cross our paths. God calls us to be
an example to others—no matter our age.

Being an example doesn't mean we have to be perfect. No one is. But,
with God's help, we will be able to show other people what it looks like
to live a life dedicated to Christ. When we love others, choose our words
carefully, make wise choices, and live in purity, we will be role models for
those who might be watching.

Who in your life might be looking at you as an example?

What could you do this week to be a better influence?

True beauty tip: Be a role model for those around you.

Day 29

LEARNING TO FEAR THE LORD

The eyes of the LORD are on those who fear him,
on those whose hope is in his unfailing love. . . .
We wait in hope for the LORD;
he is our help and our shield.

PSALM 33:18, 20

WE OFTEN THINK that fearing the Lord means being afraid and cowering before Him—like a guilty person in front of a powerful judge. It's true that fearing God means we stand in awe before Him because we recognize how powerful and holy He is. Yet fearing God also involves trusting Him. We don't need to be afraid of Him because we know His character. He is great, but He also is good. He is powerful, but He also is full of love. He is holy and perfect, but He also came to earth in human form so He could be our Savior.

For me, fearing the Lord meant realizing that God deserved to be in control of every aspect of my life—not just in what I did outside of modeling. It meant that I had to let Him take His rightful spot as Lord of my life. I had to let go of my attempts to run my own life and learn to rely on Him completely.

When we fear the Lord and put all our hope in Him, we don't have to fear anything else.

How do you view God? Do you see Him as Someone to fear or Someone to trust?

What is one change you need to make to let God be in control of your life?

True beauty tip: *Trust in the Lord and in His love.*

Day 30
THE LASTING REWARD

Charm is deceptive, and beauty is fleeting;
> but a woman who fears the LORD is to be praised.
Honor her for all that her hands have done,
> and let her works bring her praise at the city gate.

PROVERBS 31:30-31

I THOUGHT I'D RECEIVED the greatest possible reward when I won the Victoria's Secret Runway Angel competition. I had professional success, money, and lots of attention, but it didn't take me long to realize it all was hollow. The rewards I've gained since I went public with my decision to quit modeling have been totally different—and far more satisfying.

As I've shared my story about how God has worked in my life, one of my greatest privileges has been encouraging the girls and young women I've met along the way. I want them to be able to accept the way God made them and to pursue the inner beauty that comes from following Him. Those rewards are worthwhile because they're rewards that will last.

This passage from Proverbs 31 says that a woman who fears the Lord will receive praise, but this isn't the shallow praise that comes from looking a certain way. It's genuine, heartfelt appreciation from those who have been touched by our lives and have seen our love for God affect everything we do. No matter how hard we work at our appearance, physical beauty will fade with time. But no one can take away the inner beauty that comes from loving God and loving others. That's a reward that will last forever.

What rewards are you most focused on receiving?

What's one thing you can change in your life to concentrate on inner beauty?

True beauty tip: The best reward comes from loving God.

ACKNOWLEDGMENTS

FIRST AND FOREMOST, I'd like to thank my Savior, Jesus Christ. I know that none of this would have been possible without Him. He is the reason for all the good things in my life.

As in all areas of my life, the Lord guided me through the process of publishing this book. I'm thankful for the help of the people at Tyndale House Publishers: my editor, Stephanie Rische, as well as Karin Buursma, Maria Eriksen, and Andrea Martin. I owe a special thanks to Carol Traver, who was by my side every day on this amazing journey. Her support, thoughtfulness, and hard work went way beyond anything I could have asked for. Her kind and loving heart has impacted me greatly!

I am grateful to my literary agent, Chip MacGregor of MacGregor Literary, who lifted this book in prayer from the very beginning. His support and guidance are much appreciated.

I'd like to thank Michelle Medlock Adams for seeing the potential in my story, introducing me to my literary agent, and helping me take the first steps toward getting published.

There have been many people in my life who have offered me Christlike advice and helped me on my journey in writing this book, and I am grateful for them. I'm thankful for Pastor Chris Miller of Grace Church Kalispell for speaking truth into my life. The Lord has really used your biblically sound messages to convict my heart and help me to see the true condition of my heart outside of God's grace.

Special thanks to Peggy Sue Miller, Jennifer Maltby, and Yolanda Balls for living lives above reproach and for being godly examples for me. You have helped me to see what a Proverbs 31 wife looks like in the way you honor and respect your husbands.

My sincere appreciation goes out to all the individuals who have encouraged me and prayed for me through all of this. I can only hope that this book will be a blessing to you and that all the glory will be for the Lord, not for myself.

I could not have done this without the support of my family and my husband's family. Thank you all for your uplifting prayers, your encouraging support, and your unending love.

I am so grateful for my husband, Mike. His faithfulness and Christlike love have softened my heart. The seeds he has sown in my life are always at work and can be seen throughout the pages of this book. He has been 100 percent supportive of me in everything, and I could not have asked for a better friend and partner.